CHURCHES OF OLD NEW ENGLAND

Their Architecture and Their Architects
Their Pastors and Their People

THE MACMILLAN COMPANY
NEW YORK · BOSTON · CHICAGO · DALLAS
ATLANTA · SAN FRANCISCO
MACMILLAN AND CO., LIMITED
LONDON · BOMBAY · CALCUTTA · MADRAS
MELBOURNE
THE MACMILLAN COMPANY
OF CANADA, LIMITED
TORONTO

CHURCH OF THE FIRST PARISH (1816) *Lancaster, Massachusetts*
Designed by Charles Bulfinch

CHURCHES
OF *Old New England*

Their Architecture and Their Architects,
Their Pastors and Their People

By GEORGE FRANCIS MARLOWE

Illustrated with Photographs by
SAMUEL CHAMBERLAIN

THE MACMILLAN COMPANY
New York 1947

First Printing

PRINTED IN THE UNITED STATES OF AMERICA

ACKNOWLEDGMENTS

OF THE many references consulted in searching for accounts of these old New England meetinghouses and their stories, I am most indebted to the two volumes of the Reverend Henry Wilder Foote's "Annals of King's Chapel"—in actual fact a history not only of the Chapel but of all the early New England churches and of the New England colonies. These have now been supplemented and brought up to date by Dr. John Carroll Perkins's delightful third volume. Enough praise cannot be given to Dr. Weis's "The Colonial Clergy and the Colonial Churches of New England," a tremendous piece of work, invaluable to all interested in the early life of the colonies, for two hundred years ever involved in the affairs of the churches. Naturally most of the material is to be found in those many town histories so painstakingly compiled and transcribed from early church and town records by local historians. Many valuable accounts of old meetinghouses and churches have appeared in *Old Time New England,* the bulletin of the Society for the Preservation of New England Antiquities, and among these the Reverend Charles A. Place's four articles on New England meetinghouses are of great interest. At many of the churches visited I found leaflets giving in brief the more important historical facts and stories or anecdotes connected with the church. Most of these are unsigned, and to their unknown authors I wish to express much appreciation.

I am indebted to Charles Scribner's Sons for permission to quote from the late Arthur Train's "Puritan's Progress," the Houghton Mifflin Company for lines from Celia Thaxter's poem, the Atlantic Monthly Press for the quotation from James Truslow Adams "The Founding of New England" and to Macmillan and Company for that from Thomas Hardy's "The Three Strangers."

To attempt to say anything of Mr. Chamberlain's part in this book would be merely presumptuous. His remarkable photographs of scenes in New England and elsewhere are well known. The truly magnificent etchings and drawings of the French cathedrals and other European architecture made in the happy interval between the wars are unequaled by the work of any other American artist, and by few, if any, in Europe. That many of the subjects are now either terribly mutilated or entirely destroyed makes these graphic records of the great art of the Middle Ages beyond price.

After three years of highly specialized active service in Africa, Italy, and on other battle fronts in Europe, Major Chamberlain has returned and made these illustrations and designed the format of the book.

G. F. M.

FRAMINGHAM CENTRE
January, 1947

CONTENTS

ILLUSTRATIONS

CHURCHES OF OLD NEW ENGLAND

Their Architecture and Their Architects
Their Pastors and Their People

I

INTRODUCTION

DURING the later years of the eighteenth century and the first quarter of the nineteenth the New England meetinghouse attained a certain perfection of architectural elegance and grace scarcely surpassed by any other buildings of the period.

It has been the custom to describe all the work of this time as "Colonial," including many buildings of the years after the Revolution, for which Early Republic or Federal would be a more correct term.

A great part of the architectural merit of the churches and other buildings of this period lies in their nearly perfect adaptability to the materials and methods of construction available to their builders, as much as in any conscious effort in their design. Their architecture is essentially an architecture of wood, or wood and brick. Stone buildings of the seventeenth and eighteenth centuries are comparatively few. Stone was hard to quarry, and even bricks had to be made, or brought from England. But there seldom was any attempt to reproduce in wood the monumental stone architecture of the English designers. Much of the beauty of our own early work is due to a refinement and delicacy of scale. Columns and capitals, cornices and other architectural members and their moldings, though adhering to classic precedent, are all reduced to a scale suited to the material. As to the "Modernists' " opinion of these adapted classic forms, we might be more sympathetic had they not so signally failed to offer anything more satisfying or beautiful. Though some were plain, boxy little meetinghouses, with a low and rather ugly belfry, the ingenuity and variety displayed by their architects or architect-builders in ringing changes on varying compositions of columned or pilastered front, tower and belfry, cupola or spire, were seemingly unlimited, and no two churches exactly alike are to be found.

The early buildings of the seventeenth century, such as the "Old Ship" at Hingham, were simple meetinghouses in very fact and nothing more; square in plan with hipped or pitched roof, perhaps with a porch but sometimes without tower or belfry of any kind. Inside they were at first unplastered, with rough benches for seats. It was not until nearly the time of the outbreak of the Revolution that the meetinghouse plan gave way to the church plan. The first of marked architectural merit was Christ Church in Boston.

The spires of some of the later buildings, notably those of the Park Street Church in Boston and the First Baptist Meetinghouse in Providence quite evidently were inspired by some of the London churches such as St. Mary-le-Bow and St. Bride's, now destroyed by Nazi bombs. Others were adapted from books of design such as James Gibbs's "Book of Architecture." There is no spire in America, popular belief to the contrary, actually copied from one of Wren's. How great has been the loss to the world by the destruction of Wren's London churches and other old buildings only those who knew and loved old London and its ancient architecture possibly can appreciate. Sixteen of his churches alone are but shells. "The beautiful interiors," said James Bone in "London Today," "some with Grinling Gibbons carvings, all with something precious in carved wood or wrought ironwork or marble fonts or precious brasses, are gone and lost to us; they are as far from us now as the old Gothic London churches that Samuel Pepys lamented when his London went up in flames. With the exception of the building of William and Mary College at Williamsburg, Virginia, Wren never made a design for any building in the colonies.

The frames, mostly of oak, of many of the early wooden buildings were put together on the ground, and raised completely assembled. Town and other records of the Brimfield and Mendon churches describe the operation. The heavy oak timbers were fastened with wooden pins. Iron-pointed "pike poles" were provided, and as the timbers sometimes were ten or twelve inches square, large crews of men must have been required to raise them. The roof trusses in some cases probably weighed as much as four or five tons. For raising these, a simple derrick or shears with tackle and falls operated by a windlass or capstan were used, and a screw jack

—no better mechanical aid than the builders of Solomon's Temple had. Sometimes horses or oxen were used on the tackle and falls or capstan. Just how the wooden steeples were raised, we are not sure. We know from contemporary accounts and records that some of them were put together on the ground, and J. Frederick Kelly has worked out an interesting possible method with diagrams illustrating this. The rebuilt spire of Shrewsbury church, blown off in the 1938 hurricane, was replaced in a similar manner.

It must be admitted that the interiors of many of the meeting-houses are bare and uninspiring. No doubt this was largely due to the Puritan's aversion to anything that smacked of prelacy and ritualism and the Church of England. Probably they were well suited to the temperament and austere creed of their builders. In the earlier buildings and many of the later ones, the congregation faces a blank wall before which stands a reading desk which serves as pulpit. In front of this in early times were the "deacons' seat" and table. Later, when some of the amenities of life began to enter into our ancestors' way of living, and greater wealth permitted more lavish expenditure, the interiors of the churches kept pace with the more elaborate architectural treatment of the exterior. Columns, usually of the simple Doric order, supported the galleries, their balustrades more or less elaborated with paneled fronts and molded rails. But the dominating feature was the high pulpit and reading desk which came into vogue about the time of the Revolution. Curving stairs on either side gave opportunity for a mahogany handrail with turned balusters, and a crimson cushion for the reading desk and Bible gave a much needed touch of color.

The interiors of the later buildings of the Church of England, with their altar and chancel rails, their high pulpits and sounding-boards, of course were of much greater interest architecturally. Some of these had beautiful chandeliers of brass or crystal suspended by rods with ornamental wrought ironwork. These later and more monumental buildings, notably King's Chapel and Christ Church in Boston, indicate the marked influence of Wren's and other English churches such as St. James's, Piccadilly, and St. Bride's. The interior of King's Chapel is the interior of an old London church, lacking only in the elaboration of ornament and rich carving in oak and lime wood, of Grinling Gibbons and other master craftsmen of the time.

After 1825, "the heavy hand of classic formalism" fell upon New England church architecture as upon civic buildings and domestic architecture throughout the country. Then came the era of the Greek revival with its overheavy columns and other details, and reproductions in wood of Greek temples sprang up throughout New England and the Middle States and farther south. Some of these are good and have a character and charm of their own. But they were followed by the wooden pseudo-Gothic with its hollow buttresses and wooden tracery and all the cheap machine-made woodwork of the later years of the nineteenth century and since. The cunning brain and hand of the old carpenter and builder were dead, his work to be succeeded by the cheap products of the local "mill." Lost or laid away in their old chests in the attic or in the rooms of the local historical society are the old hand tools: the adzes which hewed the heavy oak timbers; the drawknives, the old wooden jack planes, and the molding planes with carefully ground knives which made the paneling and beautiful mantels, delicately molded cornices, and capitals of columns.

Most of the old churches lack really musical bells. In 1911, according to Dr. Arthur H. Nichols, seventy-eight of Paul Revere's bells were still in use. Most of them, "powerful and mellow," probably are better than any others except a very few modern ones. Dr. Nichols estimated that the Reveres, father and son, cast nearly four hundred bells between 1792 and 1826. Of those still in use, the majority were badly hung and improperly rung, and forty-seven were cracked. About forty had been destroyed by fires—a sad comment on the high rate of mortality from this cause among the old churches. Two had been struck by lightning. Where are all the others?

Though some of our city bells are now silent, in many a New England village today the sound of the church bell coming over the hills awakens pleasant memories, perhaps not without a twinge of conscience, in the breast of the Sunday motorist hurrying by; and to the exile from war-torn Europe, what thoughts of the ancient parish church in some English village, some medieval church in northern France, or the bells in the campanile on an Italian hilltop? When, in England, after more than four years of silence, the church bells were rung again, there was great rejoicing.

Today in some of the smaller towns and villages the big meetinghouse stands abandoned or used as a town hall or even a picture house. Either a smaller church has been built, or the congregation has united with some other church. Perhaps with modern transport two sections of the town have come together. As with the little red or white schoolhouse, this may be merely in the interest of efficiency, but more often it is apt to mean the gradual depopulation of our rural communities which has been going on for many years, or lack of interest in the church as an institution and a consequent decline in spiritual values. Perhaps both.

Only about a third of the *Mayflower's* passengers were of that first little group which had sought freedom in Leyden. The others, says James Truslow Adams, were "a very mixed lot." Those who came from Leyden were mostly without means for financing such an expedition, and had it not been for capital subscribed in London there would have been no settlement. And in other settlements, a large proportion were mere adventurers, looking for that financial prosperity in the New World which they had failed to find in the Old.

It is hard to realize today that Massachusetts once actually had a state church, as much a part of the civil government as was the Established Church in England. Church membership was an absolute requirement for voting. It was not until about 1826, when by law, church, and town affairs in Massachusetts were separated, that the church parishes were organized. Before that time, in all the records of church matters it will be seen that "the Town voted," and in all cases of controversy in the church the General Court was invoked as the final authority. Up to the early years of the nineteenth century, church matters in common with other business were decided in town meeting, and all accounts of them are involved with other town records.

Though we have long been told that the Puritans came for religious freedom and to escape persecution, they immediately established an oligarchy of their own, no less bent upon forcing their own will upon others than were the King and the Archbishop in England.

By the Massachusetts colonists' interpretation of the laws under the royal charter revoked in 1684, membership in the Congregational Church was a requisite for voting, although their insistence upon this actually was illegal under the charter. "For half a century," says Adams, "the leaders and the old church party had resisted, by every means in their power,—by fraud, trickery, and bloodshed, as well as by legitimate influence,—the granting of a voice in the government to any individual who could not be counted upon to uphold the power and authority" of the clergy and the church. In Lynn, in 1648, Obadiah Holmes of Newport was given thirty lashes on his bare back with a three-lash whip because he refused to pay a fine of thirty pounds for professing the doctrines of the Baptists. Persecution of the Quakers was even more relentless.

And yet those holding church membership constituted only about a quarter or a fifth of the voters. The Nonconformist struggle was not for toleration but for control. Though the new charter of 1691 "had definitely ended the legalized control of the Congregational church, [it] was still to maintain a privileged position" for another hundred and twenty-five years or more. The members of the government under the new charter, thanks to the efforts of Increase Mather in England, were nearly all of the clerical party. Mather's son, Cotton Mather, wrote in his diary: "The time for Favour was now come; the sett Time was come! . . . all the Councellors of the Province are of my own Father's Nomination; and my Father-in-law, with several related unto me, and several Brethren of my own church, are among them." Truly, "the Tyranny of the Lord-Bishops had merely been exchanged for that of the Lord-Brethren." Above all, "they would share no white surplice with Romish priest, but would minister in the scholar's black gown of Geneva." Only hell they were ever willing to share with their opponents. "They cannot quite refuse to sing; but there shall be no instrument save the human voice and such rough psalmody as was supplied to the Puritans of Amsterdam by Henry Ainsworth . . ." Their tunes were some ten in number, oftenest York, Hackney, Windsor, St. Mary, and St. Martyn's.

Cotton Mather was said to have attributed all the colony's troubles to the presence of the Church of England congregation of King's Chapel, and the Governor and Council wrote to England "pointing out that the whole disaster" of Phips's failure to capture Quebec "must have been due to God, who had 'spit in our faces' —a phrase for a state paper," says Adams, "which darts a vivid light, in several directions, among the colony's elect."

It cannot be denied that these early Puritans in the intensity of their faith were mightily pleased with themselves. "God sifted a whole nation," wrote Stoughton, "that he might send choice grain over into this wilderness." In the town records of Milford, Connecticut, for 1640, we find: "Voted, that the earth is the Lord's and the fullness thereof; Voted, that the earth is given to the Saints; Voted, that we are the Saints."

At the time of King Philip's War the Massachusetts General Court decided that the Deity had so afflicted them, and "that He was then engaged in burning towns and murdering women and children along the frontier because Massachusetts had become somewhat lax in persecuting the Quakers, and because men had begun to wear periwigs and their women to indulge in 'cutting and curling and immodest laying out of their haire.' "

The Puritans were marooned in a little world of their own, far from any of the normal interests or distractions of the life they had left behind them, and it is not surprising that seemingly trivial matters should have loomed large. And if they often were guilty of many of the weaknesses of the flesh, perhaps some of these could be condoned also. The amount of spirituous liquor consumed on every and all occasions at times seems unbelievable; whether it was a wedding or a baptism, when the poor little "saint" was starting out in life, or the funeral at the end when at last he had left it; at the raising of the frame for the new meetinghouse or the installation of the new minister, there were toddy and punch by the bowl and rum by the barrel. Nor was the cup that cheered but could scarcely have failed to inebriate confined to these special festivities. Yet, when we realize what they must have suffered in houses practically unheated, we may be glad that John Jenner was acquitted, "itt appearing to be of infirmyty and occasioned by the extremyty of the colde." And what pain and misery they endured without dentists and often without doctors! Of dentists there were none, and the doctor probably had less knowledge of human ills than the modern veterinary. There were no anesthetics of any kind—the unfortunate patient in the surgeon's hands was merely bucked up with a shot of rum.

Compared with the beautiful and often truly magnificent parish churches these people had left behind them in the Old World, with all their wealth of painted glass and carving in stone and wood, the heritage of five hundred years, these plain and bare and unadorned little buildings of New England seem of comparatively little architectural interest. Yet in their unspoiled village environment many of them are altogether charming, and those of the best period perhaps scarcely could have been improved upon. And they were well suited to the austere creeds of their congregations.

Generally the early settlers had an eye for a pleasant site. Again and again they would brave the cold sweep of winter winds on a hilltop for the sake of a broad outlook on the world below. And though some of their old burying grounds are sadly forlorn and neglected, on their leaning, moss-grown stones the knowing may read many a romantic tale of early New England life. Some of these old slate stones are pathetically small, with only a name and date. Others, adorned with crudely carved hourglass or grotesque face and marking the grave of some local celebrity—doctor of divinity or officer of the Indian wars or the Revolution, are of truly imposing proportions, with long eulogies of the deceased and his many virtues in the pompous language considered indispensable in a proper epitaph of the time. But what is the true story of the two old slate stones in the churchyard at Little Compton in Rhode Island? One is "In memory of Lydia, wife of Mr. Simeon Palmer who died Decr ye 26th 1754 in ye 35th year of her age"; the other, "In memory of Elizabeth who should have been the wife of Mr. Simeon Palmer," who died sixteen years later, having lived on into her sixty-fourth year. Many years ago Dr. William Allen Knight gave a fictional version of the story in a little book he called "St. Abigail of the Pines."

Only a part of such tales of old New England have ever been told, and between the covers of dim and faded and misspelt parish records there lies many a tale of romance and adventure; rich material for the future "Great American Novel." And as one reads the annals of the later years and the time of the Revolution approaches, one begins to suspect that there was more to be said for the Loyalist cause than our old schoolbooks would have us believe.

This is far from being an exhaustive account of all the early meetinghouses and churches in New England with a claim to architectural merit and historic interest. Such an account would run into many volumes. There are many others worthy of being included, some of which we shall no doubt pass along the way. The order herein given is an arbitrary one, and perhaps few will care to attempt to follow it throughout. But, for those sufficiently interested to visit some of these old meetinghouses and churches, perhaps not the least of the pleasure will be in traveling our fair New England country: through the green farm lands and over the rolling hills of Massachusetts and Connecticut; among the lakes and streams of lower New Hampshire and the Green Mountains of Vermont; by the Ipswich marshes and old Newbury into Maine, and southward to Narragansett Bay and Providence and historic old Newport.

If in the pages following there may seem to have been a tendency to emphasize the frailties and weaknesses of the flesh of the early New Englanders who built these meetinghouses and churches and preached and worshiped in them, at the expense of some of their more conventional Christian virtues, it has been merely because at times these same traits, often not wholly devoid of humor, seem the more outstanding in a people whom it has long been the fashion to characterize as ultrasanctimonious and pious. Yet one writer has described them as "these merriest of Puritans."

II

BOSTON: THE OLD SOUTH AND KING'S CHAPEL

GRANDEST of all, perhaps, of our old Puritan meetinghouses, is the Old South. Its tower doorway stands at the very edge of the sidewalk, yet how many in the hurrying crowds in Washington Street who pass it daily have ever stepped aside to cross the threshold? To most Bostonians it is just the "Old South," vaguely thought of as having had something to do with the early history of the town, perhaps to be shown some day to a visitor, like the Old State House and Faneuil Hall and Bunker Hill Monument. Yet Faneuil Hall itself has not witnessed more stirring scenes or events, and to fully write this church's history would be to write the history of Boston and New England.

Surrounded and overshadowed by the tall buildings in Washington and Milk streets, the little structure seems modest and unimposing, though its spire has been extravagantly praised. But, passing the inner vestibule, one is surprised at the impressive size and scale of the interior. Facing the Milk Street side, now no longer used as an entrance, is the imposing high pulpit with ornamental cornice and frieze carried on engaged Corinthian columns at the corners, with mahogany rostrum beneath a great hanging sounding board. Two tiers of balustraded and ornamented galleries on either side are carried on fluted columns. Unfortunately, modern chairs have taken the place of the old box pews, only four of which have been preserved. Here are portraits of Boston worthies of the past, old prints, and other views of scenes connected with the history of the town and cases of various articles of antiquarian or artistic interest.

Having barely escaped destruction in the great fire of 1872, which stopped at the opposite corner of Milk and Washington streets, the building was used as a post office for a time; and in 1876 it was auctioned off for junk. The congregation had moved to the monumental but not particularly appropriate Italianate building at the newly laid-out Copley Square, and, though among them were some of Boston's most opulent citizens, the historic old church was left to its fate. But a group of patriotic women got together and undertook to raise the necessary funds. In spite of all efforts, the option was about to expire when Mrs. Mary Hemenway made up the amount with the largest subscription of all, and the building was saved—a fitting memorial for that centennial year of Independence. The full amount, $400,000, was not raised until later, when the church was restored as nearly as possible to its condition at the time of the Revolution. The present pulpit, restored in 1909, was built in 1808, replacing that installed when the building was repaired in 1783. The exterior paint was removed in 1913, when other repairs and restorations were made.

This was the site of Governor Winthrop's last dwelling place—the Governor's Green, as it was called—which extended along the "High Waye" between Spring Lane and Milk Street. The house stood on the northerly part, facing the garden. Some years after the Governor's death in 1649, house and land came into the possession of John Norton, the minister of the First Church. He died in 1663, and when dissent arose over the terms of the Covenant and the Third Church was organized his widow gave the garden plot for the new meetinghouse; later she gave the rest of the Green and the house for a parsonage. The house was so used until the winter of 1775–76, when the British soldiers pulled it down during the siege for use as firewood.

The first meetinghouse of the Third Church was built in 1669—a little house of cedar with a steeple, and porches on the front and two sides. This was the church of the years of the royal governors and of John and Cotton Mather and of Judge Sewall; and here Benjamin Franklin—born on the other side of Milk Street—was baptized on the day of his birth, January 6 (Old Style), 1706. It became known as the Old South in distinction from the New South Church built in 1717 in Summer Street on the site still known as Church Green.

In August, 1635, thirty-four years before the formation and building of the Third Church, there had been a terrific gale along the New England coast. A vessel with twenty-three people on board was wrecked on Cape Ann. All were lost except two,

Anthony Thacher and his wife, who were somehow cast ashore. Their nephew, who had been on board, by some "melancholy forebodings" had left the ship at Ipswich. Thus was the young Thomas Thacher remarkably preserved to become the first minister of the Old South Church.

Sir Edmund Andros, the Royal Governor, on his arrival in Boston in 1686, demanded that one of the meetinghouses be given over for Church of England services; and Randolph, the King's commissioner, was sent to get the key of the Old South. Though a committee of which Judge Sewall was one waited upon the Governor to protest, it was in vain. Services were held there the following Sunday and through the next two years, until the erection of King's Chapel. The Old South congregation meanwhile had to wait for their service until the English Church service was over.

It has been the custom to describe Andros as a "tyrant," fit representative of a despotic master. But the colonists had just lost their charter, and under the circumstances any royal governor was likely to be hated. Henry Cabot Lodge, in his later years at any rate no friend to foreign alliances, said: "Andros was not only a man of character, but he seems to have been personally above reproach, . . . a good administrator who served a stupid and oppressive King."

Lady Andros, the Governor's American wife, died less than three months after their arrival, and her funeral was held in the Old South Church at night by the light of candles and flaming torches. Soldiers lined the way from the Governor's mansion to the church, and from here she was taken in a hearse drawn by six horses, with the procession lighted by torch bearers, to the tomb in the First (King's Chapel) Burying Ground.

It was in this first little wooden building in 1696 that Judge Samuel Sewall stood up before the congregation while his confession was read that he had been wrong in admitting certain "spectral evidence" at the witchcraft trials, leading to the conviction of innocent persons. And it was not until seventeen years later that Cotton Mather wrote in his diary the admission that he was in error when he preached that sermon which had done much to incite the witch trials. "I entreated the Lord that I might understand the meaning of the Descent from the Invisible World which

OLD SOUTH MEETINGHOUSE (1729) *Boston, Massachusetts*

nineteen years ago produced a sermon from me, a good part of which is now published."

Sewall, Cotton, and Mather! What names in the history of early New England! So said President Oakes at Harvard when Cotton Mather took his degree, referring to Mather's grandfathers. We are apt to think of them together. Only a few days after he had been ordained, Cotton Mather attended a "private Fast" at Sewall's house. On this occasion, after three other clergymen had alternately prayed and preached, "Mr. Moody prayed about an hour and half." Then they sang the Seventy-ninth Psalm and distributed "some Biskets & Beer, Cider, Wine. The Lord hear in Heaven his dwelling place."

Cotton Mather declared wine to be a gift of God, and consumed a lot of it.

The forty years and more of Sewall's life with his first wife were particularly happy ones. The story of his marriage with the mintmaster's daughter has been told many times, and Hannah's death was undoubtedly the great sadness and misfortune of his life. But widows and widowers were expected to remarry in those days. He had written William Dennison's will and attended his funeral, and during the next nine months he paid frequent visits to the widow at Roxbury, riding either on horseback (when he presented her with shoe buckles) or "in the coach." But in spite of other presents—including cases of cutlery which he carefully notes cost 4s. 6d. and a "pound of raisins with proportional almonds"—the lady decided elsewhere. Sewall wrote: "My bowels yearn toward Mrs. Dennison; but I think God directs me in his Providence to desist."

Just two years and ten days after his first wife's death, the Judge, now Chief Justice of Massachusetts and with children and grandchildren, married Mrs. Tilly. His son Joseph performed the ceremony. His life with this lady was short, however, for she died suddenly in the following May; and once more the widower, now seventy-three years old, began to look about him. Four months later he notes: "Saturday I dine at Mr. Stoddard's; from thence to Madam Winthrop's just at three. . . . Had a pleasant discourse" with her about "seven single persons sitting in the Fore Seat" of the Old South Meetinghouse. Joseph Sewall was then the colleague of the minister, Ebenezer Pemberton, and if he chanced to be

fin's Wharf and the harbor. Paul Revere was somewhere in the crowd.

Two years later, when on the fifth anniversary of the Boston Massacre the inhabitants dared the indignation of General Gage, the church again was crowded to the doors. British officers arrived early and were conducted to seats with meticulous civility; but in spite of the thick sprinkling of scarlet coats the meeting went on. The church was so full that when Joseph Warren, the orator of the day, arrived he could reach his place only by climbing a ladder placed at a window back of the pulpit. The story is that a young ensign was assigned to throw an egg at Warren if he went too far in the denunciation of the royal authority, as a signal to break up the meeting; but on the way to the church the ensign chosen stubbed his toe and fell, dislocating his knee and breaking the egg. In spite of sudden confusion at the end, when someone's shout of "Fie, fie!" was taken for a cry of "Fire," and some of the crowd rushed to the windows and managed to climb down to the street, there seems to have been surprisingly good behavior on both sides. But the British had their revenge, for during the occupation and siege Burgoyne had the pews torn out and the floor covered with gravel, and the church was used as a riding rink by the regiment of the Queen's Light Dragoons. One pew was left for a pigsty.

Since the days when Washington Street was Marlborough Street, the tower clock of the brick church has been steadily ticking off the hours. The Reverend Thomas Prince, ordained as colleague of Joseph Sewall in 1718 and the leading New England antiquary of the time, used a room in the tower for his study; and here he deposited his New England library, a priceless collection of books and manuscripts. Among other treasures was Governor Bradford's "History of Plimoth Plantation," which found its way to the Bishop of London's palace at Fulham, in after years to be returned to Boston and kept at the State House. During the occupancy of the British, many of Prince's books and manuscripts were us[illegible] kindling for the stove which had been set up in the church.

[illegible]hough Judge Sewall didn't live long enough to see much [illegible]w meetinghouse it is the figure of old Samuel that we [illegible]see in a pew as we enter the gathering gloom of the old [illegible]n on a winter's afternoon, in his black gown and white neck-[illegible]oth, his long white hair reaching to his shoulders (in defiance of "periwigs"): that New England Pepys who in his diary draws aside the curtain to reveal to us the most intimate pictures of life in old Boston and New England.

At the corner of Tremont and School streets stands that old stone fort still known as King's Chapel; built, one would think, to stand siege by all the powers of Puritanism and Nonconformity in New England. "The Royal Chapel," Thomas Harward called it, when writing to the Bishop of London in 1731. Yet it ultimately gave way before those changes in religious thought and doctrine which swept over the country soon after the Revolution, and the first Episcopal church in New England became the first Unitarian church in America.

Though both buildings are of the eighteenth century, King's Chapel, most English of all our old New England churches, was as appropriate to the regime of the royal governors and Episcopacy as the Old South was to that of the Puritans; and, in spite of the grim and forbidding aspect of the Chapel's granite walls, if Harrison's design had been completed, the tower and spire and other intended details would have given the exterior the added grace and elegance characteristic of Wren's London churches. Of the beautiful interior, enough cannot be said. It stands out among all our old churches of the Church of England plan as opposed to the Puritan meetinghouse. More than the exterior, it has the atmosphere of an old London church, and it is but little changed today from the way Harrison left it. But for the Revolution with all the attendant difficulties and misfortunes, the interior would have been of stone instead of wood; but we scarcely regret the loss, so beautiful are the paired columns with their finely carved Corinthian capitals, the organ in its old case, unchanged (even the royal crown and episcopal mitres have been restored), the shallow chancel and its reredos with the tablets of the law, the Lord's Prayer, and the Apostles' Creed; the fine pulpit and sounding board. The royal governor's pew with its crimson draperies, once surmounted by the royal crown, has been restored. In 1826 this was removed, a sacrifice to an iconoclastic age and New England thrift, in order, as Josiah Quincy said, "that two plebeian pews might be constructed upon its ample site," and sold—probably to the highest bidder. "It stood handsomely out, with ornamented pillars at the corners. . . . I came too late into the world to see a royal governor enter this august pew; though the ghosts of some of them would occasionally seem to steal up the aisle and creep into it during the drowsier passages of the afternoon sermon; but the flesh-and-blood personage who occupied the pew in my day was, so to speak, as good a governor as the best of them. He was a son of a Massachusetts governor too; and, surely, there could be no better ideal of those royal qualities which should characterize the ruler of a State than was presented in the Federal leader, William Sullivan. How that pew of royal dignity used fairly to blossom with the large and lovely family of which he was the head!" Sullivan's monument is on the south wall. It was Mr. Foote's earnest wish when rector to have the state pew restored and the escutcheons which once had hung upon the walls reproduced and hung again in their former places.

As the history of the Old South is the history of Puritan Boston and Massachusetts, so that of King's Chapel is a chronicle of that portion of the community which stood most firmly for loyalty to Church and King. With the completion and publication nearly fifty years ago of the more than twelve hundred pages of the Reverend Henry Wilder Foote's "Annals," the mass of available material became almost overwhelming. One is tempted to quote from every page; every chapter is material for a romance. The list of pew holders is a small New England edition of "Burke" and the names of their descendants fill a good part of the Boston "Blue Book." Memories of families long famous in Boston, among them many well known and prominent today, return to people these ancient pews. Among them a leading place surely belongs to Charles Apthorp, twice warden and treasurer of the building committee of the present Chapel and a generous subscriber. How we should like to see him and his wife Grizel as with most of their eighteen children they walked down the aisle to their double pew, fifth from the front on the right of the center and running through from aisle to aisle. His eldest daughter married a son of Alexander Hamilton.

As we have seen, the first little wooden church was built in 1688, practically upon the orders of Governor Andros. Attempts had been made to buy a piece of Sewall's land on Cotton Hill—with what results may be imagined. "I told him [Captain Davis]

KING'S CHAPEL (1749)
Designed by Peter Harrison

Boston, Massachusetts

. . . would not put Mr. Cotton's land to such an use, and besides 'twas entail'd. . . . I would not set up that wch ye People of New England came over to avoid." Whereupon the Governor and Council asserted their authority and appropriated the corner of the old burying ground at Tremont and School streets, next to the schoolhouse. Though this aroused great indignation, the right to do so being hotly disputed, it is probable that the Governor and Council, as the only lawful authorities at the time, had the right to convey a piece of the public land; and not even Sewall has recorded any valid attempt to annul the conveyance.

The only view we have of this first little church, taken from an old print of Boston of about 1720, shows it as a wooden building with two rows of three windows at the sides and the east end, and a plain square tower, the whole capped by a four-sided shingled roof. Above this a tall pole or finial rises to a most remarkable height, apparently nearly as high as the beacon on Beacon Hill which appears in the background. About halfway up, the pole is encircled by a royal crown, while as high again above the tower roof the immense cock which forms the weathervane seems to lord it over the surrounding housetops. At this time Tremont Street was a lane traversed by cows going to pasture on the common. Opposite the church were two or three houses, and about halfway between Beacon Street and Pemberton Square where the land rose to what was known as Cotton Hill was the estate of Judge Sewall, "distant from other buildings and very bleake," the land which Captain Davis did not get. The schoolhouse stood where the chancel and pulpit of the present church are now. Sewall wrote: " 'Tis finally said that the Church shall be set between the School House and Capt. Townsend's corner, . . . so that it may not stand just full up with Mr. Moody's gate, where it would have wholly cut off the way between my fence and John Coney's, and stood upon the cartway that is now into the [burying] ground."

Services were first held in the building on the Sunday of the 30th of June, 1689. The cost was £284. 16s., of which £256. 9s. was contributed by ninety-six persons throughout the colony and the balance was made up by Andros on his departure and by other English officers later. Andros and Randolph did not remain to enter the building they had done so much to obtain.

At first there were no pews, benches being provided for the congregation to sit on (built-in pews not coming into use until about 1712). The pulpit had a "cushion with fringe, tassel, and silk," and the escutcheons of various dignitaries which hung above their seats gave a touch of color to the otherwise bare interior.

In May, three years before, there had entered the harbor a vessel "freighted heavily with woe" according to Increase Mather; the frigate *Rose,* which brought a commission to Joseph Dudley as President of Massachusetts, Maine, Nova Scotia and "the lands between." She also brought the rector of King's Chapel, the Reverend Robert Ratcliffe, the first clergyman of the English Church with special authority to officiate in New England. The guns of the "Castle" saluted the King's ship. On landing, the newcomers "went up a short, broad street, paved with rough pebble, to the wooden market-building and town hall, . . . above the Exchange, partly open to the weather," where the Old State House now stands.

Ratcliffe was a graduate of Exeter College, Oxford, and a "very Excellent preacher" according to the bookseller Dunton.

On the morning of the 6th of June, 1686, the liturgy of the Church of England was publicly read for the first time, and nine days later, we find by the first entry in the parchment-bound folio, the earliest record book of King's Chapel, the "Church of England as by law established" was organized in Boston.

But Ratcliffe's stay was short, for with the recall of Andros on the overthrow of the Stuarts and news of the landing of William of Orange at Torbay in Devonshire, received in Boston on the 4th of April, 1689, Ratcliffe returned to England. For a while revolution had been rife. When Randolph took refuge in the fort on Fort Hill, guns were turned against it, compelling surrender. The governor was lodged in the house of a Mr. Usher, and Randolph, with some of Ratcliffe's leading parishioners, was actually kept in the old stone jail in Prison Lane from April to January, when by royal command he was sent to England. Thomas Danforth, the former Deputy Governor, wrote to Increase Mather, "We have a wolf by the ears." Meanwhile the church windows were broken, and doors and walls daubed with mud and filth.

Faithful to his charge, Ratcliffe waited for three months, probably until the arrival of his successor and the completion of the little wooden church insured the permanance of the work he had undertaken "in a climate which must have chilled his soul." On the 1st of July, 1689, Samuel Myles, son of the Baptist minister of Rehoboth, Massachusetts, read the service for the first time. He was to be the rector for nearly forty years.

Dislike of the Church of England continued to be shown, however; and the rowdy element took advantage of it. In the records for November 5, 1691, we find "To a Colecktion for mendin' ye church winders." It may be noted that this was Guy Fawkes Day, which English boys, singing,

"Remember, remember,
The fifth of November,
The Gunpowder Treason and Plot,"

have observed ever since Fawkes and his fellow conspirators attempted to blow up King James and his parliament by placing barrels of gunpowder in a cellar under the building.

The day, ever traditional for pranks and license similar to that of our Hallowe'en and the Fourth of July, was observed with especial enthusiasm in Boston, where effigies of the Pope and the Devil were carried through the streets.

A week later the same item for "mendin" appears again, and on the 24th, "Paid Mr. Tho. Messinger for winder shutters £1. 7s. 8d." And on the 26th of March following: "Paid Mr. Wheeler for 24 Squ: glas £00. 06s. 00d." Christmas services in 1695 aroused similar malice, when there was "pd. for mending windous to Conningham 18s.," while other records as late as 1700 give evidence of continued attacks. All of which doubtless was looked upon with but little displeasure by the older members of the Puritan party, who lost no opportunity to tease and harry their opponents in the Church of England. Some wag published a long broadside purporting to be an address to the King, beginning: *"May it please Your Majesty,*—We, Your Majesty's most Loyal Subjects . . . thought it needful to Represent to Your Majesty that there is a number of *Boston Boyes* who . . . Violently Assaulted our Church Windows to our unaccountable damage. . . . We therefore implore Your Majesties utmost Assistance against these Unlucky Boyes." The holding of property in proximity to a schoolhouse still continues to have its annoyances.

Sewall was always on the alert, and it must be said that his faultfinding was not always confined to the Church of England party. He writes: "Yesterday the Gov. comitted Mr. Holyoke's Almanack to me; and looking it over this morning I blotted out ag^{t} Febr. 14th, *Valentine,* March 25, *Annunciation of the B. Virgin;* Apr. 24, *Easter;* Sepr. 29, *Michaelmas;* Decr. 25, *Christmas.* Later he writes: "Mr. Nathaniel Gookin preaches in the afternoon; I think every time he mention'd *James* 'twas prefixing *Saint;* about 4 or 5 times that I took notice of. I suppose he did it to confront me, and to assert his own Liberty."

During Myles's rectorate, in 1710, the Chapel was enlarged to twice its original size. More than half the cost was subscribed by the British officers in Boston. Including the newly added galleries there were now a hundred and twenty-two pews, though they must have been small. Places were reassigned to the proprietors: each person was expected to pay for his own pew—and pay promptly. It was voted: "Unless Doc^{r}. Lake immediately pay to the Church Wardens the sum of five pounds towards the Repair of the Church, y^{t} thay dispose of the pew he Sitts in to Sutch persons as they shall See Convenant; and also any other p^{r}son or p^{r}sons y^{t} shall Refuse to pay their quotas, paying him or them ther money that was disbursed for that Use."

One of the two long pews in front of the pulpit was made into a square pew for Colonel Tailer, the Lieutenant Governor, and the two behind for the masters of vessels in the harbor. Another was set aside for eight old men. The pulpit was removed to "the next pillar" at the east, near the center of the church, and the clock given by the Gentlemen of the British Society took the place of the great brass-mounted hourglass which had stood on the pulpit.

It was at this time that the church received the gift of the famous organ from Thomas Brattle, the first ever heard in New England. Though in general practice Brattle was a Nonconformist, he was known and valued "for his Catholic Charity to all of the reformed Religion, but more especially his gr^{t} Veneration for the Ch. of Engl^{d}."

Brattle, who was an enthusiastic musician, had imported the

organ from London, and by his will had left it to the Brattle Square Church "if they shall accept thereof, and within a year after my decease procure a Sober person that can play skilfully thereon with a loud noise. Otherwise to ye Church of England in this towne on ye same terms and conditions." And the Brattle Square Church voted "that they did not think it proper to use the same in the publick worship of God." Whereupon, at a meeting of the "Gentlemen of the Church," it was voted that the "Orgains Giveing them by Thomas Brattle, Esqr: Dece^d . . . be Accepted by the Church, and that Mr Miles answer Mr William Brattle's Letter concerning the Same."

There is a tradition that when later the Brattle Square people changed their minds, a wealthy parishioner, on the arrival of an organ from England, offered to give for the poor the sum which it had cost if the boxes containing it were thrown overboard.

Our forefathers had brought from England five tunes, and these perpetuated not by printed notes but by ear alone, for a long time were the only ones in use. Cotton Mather said of the church music, "Their singing has degenerated into an odd noise that has had more of what we want a name for than any regular singing in it." Judge Sewall had a musical gift, or thought he had, and used to "set the tune" at the Old South. With his usual self-revealing frankness he tells a story on himself: "I intended Windsor, and fell into High Dutch; and then essaying to set another Tune, went a Key much too high. The Lord humble me and Instruct me that I should be occasion of any Interruption in the Worship of God."

In December, 1708, Henry Harris sailed from England to become "Lecturer" at the Queen's Chapel (as the church was called upon the accession of Queen Anne), a young, active, and vigorous clergyman who evidently had the gift of winning friends and keeping on good terms with his rector, though he was administered a severe rebuff in a controversy with the ever meddling Increase Mather and in later years his ministry was embittered by oppositions and disappointments. It was an age of pamphleteers, and Harris printed a long preface to Archbishop King's "Inventions of Men in the Worship of God," with personal allusions to Dr. Mather such as "had never before been breathed above a whisper in Boston," in which he said: "An

Eminent Nonconformist writer should have . . . corrected what is amiss in the Congregational Scheme of Government, and Method of Worship, before he laid his Charge against the most perfect Church upon Earth. . . . The letter which he has lately Reprinted is adapted to vulgar Capacities, such as cannot distinguish between Truth and Falsehood, . . . but what good it can do is difficult to conceive, unless it be good to harden People in their Hatred and Animosities . . . against the best Protestant Churches in the World." And so the warfare continued from the neighboring pulpits of Cotton Mather and Pemberton. Mather said: "One Main End of our Predecessors Coming hither was to keep their Children unacquainted with such *Foolish Customs.* To introduce them can be no *Kindness* to us. . . . *Christmas Revels* begin to be taken up among some vainer Young People here and there in some of our Towns. . . . The *Shrove-Tuesday Vanities* of making *Cakes to the Queen of Heaven,* etc."

The year following the death of Samuel Myles, there came to King's Chapel in 1729 one of the most outstanding characters of the church of that time in New England—the Reverend Roger Price, the newly appointed deputy, or "commissary," of the Bishop of London. Poor Harris did not long survive the arrival of the new rector. He died in the following October, perhaps in part of weariness and disappointment. The animosity of his opponents followed him to the grave, for the vestry voted "that no money should be paid out of the church stock towards defraying the charge" of burying him.

On the 8th of the previous January there had passed forever from the streets of Boston Judge Sewall, the old diarist who, ever poking forward that inquiring nose of his, has walked with us thus far on our journey. With his death one of the most important sources of Boston and New England history of the times was closed.

The old English system of plural benefices and livings prevailed, more or less unquestioned. On the death of his assistant, Thomas Howard, Price wrote to his brother: "I have wrote to the Bishop of London to confer the place upon me, that I may have the liberty of appointing a Curate under me who may be more dependent and servicable than the Assistant has hitherto been. The salary is a Hundred Pounds per Annum, paid out of the

Treasury, deducting something for taxes, out of which I propose to give the person that shall act under me seventy pounds per annum, certain, and the rest of the Income if he behaves himself orderly, according to his Station."

Later the same year he wrote to the Bishop: "If my assistant is not already appointed, it would be a great pleasure to me to be joined with one of my own Countrymen. I find the New England Ministers too overbearing, and to want some balance." But the church distrusted any such arrangement. After further long correspondence His Lordship of London appointed the Reverend Addington Davenport, born in Boston, who after serving the King's Chapel for three years did important service in the founding of the new Trinity Church at the corner of Summer Street and Bishop's Alley.

On the 19th of July, 1728, there arrived in Boston Governor William Burnet, son of the famous Bishop of Salisbury, and a godson of King William III. He was received in Boston "with a Splendour and Magnificence superior to what have ever been known in these Parts of the World." Salutes were fired as he entered the town, and crowds of gentlemen met him as an escort when his commission was read in the presence of the clergy and civic dignitaries. His administration was sadly short, however, for fourteen months after his arrival his carriage was overturned in the water at the ferry returning from Cambridge and he was drowned.

Mr. Commissary Price, after his marriage, lived in a house belonging to his wife's uncle, Stephen Greenleaf, the old sheriff of Suffolk under Governor Bernard. It stood in a large garden which extended from what is now Temple Place to West Street. The house afterwards became a place of public resort, known as Washington Gardens. At one time he lived on the corner of Summer and Sea streets, near Bull's Wharf, in a house which belonged to his wife. But he liked best the farm he had bought in Hopkinton, where Sir Harry Frankland and Thomas Valentine, son of one of his wardens, the King's Advocate General, and others of the "gayer and more free-living" of his parishioners had established a summer colony. Here he preached in the little church which he tried unsuccessfully to get the Society for the Propagation of the Gospel to support. Here his eldest son, Major William

Price and his daughter Elizabeth lived for many years and lie buried in the old burying-ground.

Dr. Greenwood, in his "History of King's Chapel," said of Price: "Though he had not lived on the happiest terms with his people, his talents were good and his morals irreproachable." That he could not adapt himself to the ways of New England is perhaps not surprising, "always wishing to live more like a dignitary of the Church at home than the habits of this country would bear." Price's fondness for a country residence, particularly for Hopkinton, and his time spent there, brought much criticism by the members of his congregation; perhaps not without reason. In a letter to Thomas Sandford, who seems to have acted as a sort of liaison officer between the wardens and vestry and the Bishop of London, we find: "The last Summer, when we had no other Minister, he purchased several lands at Hopkinton, about 27 Miles from Town, and ever since that has frequently resorted to that place, and still must do it as long as he holds those lands to make any benefit of them. These things are great retirements from his parochial dutys, and the furnishing of him with a Curate is not ye properest means to make him the more Steady and laborious. We might add that we did not take it kindly when he took a tour of about a month to New York to see the Countrey, without giving his Ch^h any notice of it."

Price's rectorship lasted seventeen years. In time there arose the usual dissensions and criticisms by wardens and vestry, at the last largely due to the ordination by the Bishop of London of the Reverend William Hooper and his installation as rector of the new Trinity Church. Price resigned and went to England, sailing in June of 1747, in the *Mermaid* man-of-war. Once he returned to the colonies for several years to look after his Hopkinton estate.

The congregation now resolved to choose their rector to suit themselves from among those of the Church already in New England, instead of asking the Bishop of London to send them one, and in April, 1747, the Reverend Henry Caner was inducted as the fourth rector of King's Chapel, Mr. Price assisting. Dr. Caner came to "the most conspicuous Episcopal pulpit in America" after a hard service of twenty-two years in the mission at Fairfield, Connecticut. Though the congregation did not realize it, the church was entering upon a new epoch. Dr. Caner's long and eventful ministry was cast in the troublesome times preceding the Revolution, and it was during his rectorate that the present church was built.

Strangely bare and unchurchly, the first little wooden building must have seemed to those English clergymen who had come out to the New World from beautiful college chapels and parish churches rich in carving of wood and stone both inside and out and, in spite of the devastation of two Cromwells, still retaining much of their stained glass. Yet even in Puritan New England it was still to some extent an age of color and elegance and dignity of dress. The governor in gold lace and ruffled sleeves sat in his pew beneath the royal arms, ladies and gentlemen in silks and satins, the men in powdered wigs and wearing their swords, mingled with the scarlet uniforms of British officers, while Price or Caner in cassock and bands leaned from the pulpit or read the service from the desk in the chancel. Escutcheons on the walls above their owner's pews lent a touch of color to the otherwise drab walls. At the east end was "the Altar-piece, whereon was the Glory painted, the Ten Commandments, the Lord's Prayer, the Creed and some texts of Scripture."

The establishment of Trinity Church in Summer Street and the consequent withdrawal of many of the supporters of King's Chapel was the cause of more or less hard feeling on both sides. September 18, 1740, we find the record:

"Voted, That the Church Wardens order a lock to be put on y^e door of y^e Pew No. 56 Sold to Mr Thos Hawding and to deliver the key to Mr Hawding wth Possession of y^e Said pew. At y^e Same time Agreed by the Vestry (nemine contradicente) that if Mr Thos Green should goe into y^e $afores^d$ pew, or Order any person or persons into said pew to intreupt Mr Hawding in y^e quiet possession, or disturb y^e peace of y^e Church, that the Church Wardens w^h Some of the Vestry Shall goe and warn him or them out; and if he or they are refractory they shall be turned out by force." About a month later, when "the Gentlemen of ye Vestry were . . . acquainted that Mr Thos Green had taken of the lock . . . they ordered Mr Green to be notified to meet them on Wednesday Evening next at ye Sun Tavern." An unpleasant evening probably for Mr. Green.

All this and more because Thomas Green had transferred his allegiance to Trinity Church. The pew was sold and he received £12. 10s. for his share of it. So Green won, and the Chapel lost an endowment of £500 established at Trinity Church by his heirs, now worth many times that sum. Pews seem ever to have been a cause of contention in New England churches.

Proposals for the rebuilding of the King's Chapel in stone were first made during Price's rectorate, when a subscription list was started, headed by Governor Shirley with a hundred pounds, the last on the list being Peter Faneuil, who promised two hundred. On Mr. Caner's arrival the matter was again brought up and other names added to the list, including Shirley (with another two hundred pounds), Thomas Lechmere, Frankland, Apthorp, and over a hundred more. It was not until a dozen years later, however, that Brockwell, then "King's Lecturer," was able to write to the Bishop of London that the "old Chapel" was being taken down. Two of the vestry had been instructed to "make Enquiry whether Doc^r^ Sewalls Meeting house can be Obtaine^d^ for the Chapel Congregation to Assemble in on Christmas Day," and, much to the credit of the Old South, in view of past relations, this somewhat surprising request was promptly granted; "only they Expected that wee would not decorate it with Spruce, etc." This did not meet with the approval of Brockwell, who arranged to have service in Trinity Church.

Letters were written to the King, the Archbishop of Canterbury, and others. Peter Faneuil made another large subscription, and at last, on the 11th of August, 1749, Governor Shirley laid the cornerstone. The first service was held in the incomplete building in August, 1754, but it was not brought to its present state until about eight years later. It is said to have been the first stone building in the colonies. Originally there was a balustrade around the whole building above the cornice, which must have added greatly to its appearance. This is shown in an engraving of 1833; but later it fell into decay, and unfortunately has been only partially replaced. As we have seen, the spire was never built. A beautiful new organ brought from England in 1756 was paid for by individual subscriptions. There is a tradition that this was selected by Handel, then the King's favorite musician. In 1883 parts of the organ were renewed, the old case being unchanged.

The old Brattle organ was sold to St. Paul's Church in Newburyport, where it was used for eighty years. Then it was acquired by St. John's Church, Portsmouth.

It was not until 1816 that the church had any heating other than the small tin footstoves in the pews, filled by the sexton. In November of that year a committee was appointed "to provide and erect such stoves, etc., as shall warm the church comfortably and securely." The committee seems to have been dilatory, however, for three years later "the Wardens were requested to have the second stove erected."

In spite of the ever present petty annoyances and friction with the opposing party, the first ten years of Caner's ministry, which saw the beginning and practical completion of the new church, must have been years of considerable satisfaction. But the storm was gathering, and life in Boston for the Loyalists was year by year growing more uncomfortable. "Bent with bodily infirmities and in his seventy-seventh year," wrote Mr. Foote, "his age and his position placed Dr. Caner at the head of the Church of England clergy in this part of the country. This church, too, had been attended by the officers of the British army stationed in Boston,—which had brought the old minister into yet closer bonds of sympathy and fellowship with those representatives of the King whose church he served. Their red coats were to his eyes the honored uniform of a proud service, while to the Sons of Liberty the scarlet seemed to be branded by Scripture itself as the livery of sin. Our records show abundantly the pastoral labors which devolved upon him in his relations with his military congregation. The last burials accorded by his trembling hand are those of three soldiers of his Majesty's sixty-fifth regiment of foot."

During the siege and afterwards, that portion of the population of Boston which preferred to remain loyal to King and Country suffered financial ruin and untold physical hardship. In a letter from Halifax, dated May 10, 1776, Dr. Caner describes his escape:

"As to the Clergy of Boston, indeed, they have for eleven months past been exposed to difficulty & distress in every shape; and as to myself, having determined to maintain my post as long as possible, I continued to officiate to the small remains of my parishioners, though without a support, till the 10th of March, when I suddenly and unexpectedly received notice that the King's troops would immediately evacuate the town. It is not easy to paint the distress & confusion of the inhabitants on this occasion. I had but six or seven hours allowed to prepare for this measure, being obliged to embark the same day for Halifax, where we arrived the 1st of April. This sudden movement prevented me from saving my books, furniture or any part of my interest, except bedding, wearing apparel & a little provision for my small family during the passage.

"I am now at Halifax with my daughter and servant but without any means of support, except what I receive from the benevolence of the worthy Dr Breynton."

Mr. Foote says: "No less than eighteen Episcopal clergymen from Boston and the neighborhood sailed away in the fleet that bore Dr. Caner out of Boston harbor. The town of Boston would have been left without any Episcopal clergyman at all, and consequently, (according to the theory of some), without any religious privileges at all, had it not been for the Christian charity and thoughtfulness of good Dr. Andrew Eliot, the pastor of the New North Church."

Yet, in partial atonement perhaps for the forcible possession of their meetinghouse nearly a century before, the request by the congregation of the Old South for the use of King's Chapel while their own church was being repaired, was granted.

In April, 1782, there was called to King's Chapel, first as a "reader," a young man destined to influence its future as none of his predecessors had done. The Reverend James Freeman, born in near-by Charlestown, was the son of a sea captain who had gone to Quebec as a merchant.

Freeman early began to have serious doubts about the doctrine of the Trinity. He accordingly ceased to read such parts of the liturgy as referred to it and proposed to the congregation an amended form of prayer. With the reestablishment of the Episcopal Church after the Revolution, there had of course been a certain amount of revision of the Prayer Book, omitting the prayers for the King and Royal Family and substituting others for the President of the United States and members of the government. Freeman expected that the avowal of his opinions

KING'S CHAPEL (1749) *Boston, Massachusetts*

would result in his immediate dismissal from the ministry; but Unitarianism was in the air, and in 1785 the revisions of the committee appointed for the purpose were accepted and the book was printed. The revision, largely the work of Dr. Freeman, was based upon a modified Church of England liturgy which had been prepared by the English Unitarian, Dr. Samuel Clarke, sometime rector of St. James's, Piccadilly. Despite the fact that all references to the Trinity were omitted, and the Nicene and Athanasian creeds, and that there were many other changes and abridgments, the somewhat astonishing statement was made that "this church claims never to have broken the historic chain which links it to the Anglican Church from which it sprang. . . . The alterations made in the Book of Common Prayer were not intended by ourselves, in whatever light they might be viewed by others, as a public manifestation of dissent and secession from the Church of England."

Other revisions have been made from time to time, but the King's Chapel Prayer Book is still in use. Though this book is occasionally used to some extent in other Unitarian churches, the Chapel may be said to be the only one which regularly uses the Episcopal form of service.

Dr. Freeman served the church for fifty-four years. Though now usually referred to as "ministers," the clergymen of the Chapel are still officially its "rectors."

Although Tremont Street on a Sunday in the early part of the last century would have seemed to us like a village street, to the Proprietors and Wardens of King's Chapel it apparently did not, for in 1822, with the deacons and wardens of seventeen other Boston churches they voted "to adopt measures to enforce the Law which prohibits unlawful driving on the Lord's Day" and "requested the prosecution of any person who shall drive any Carriage in School Street or Tremont Street during the time of divine service on the Lord's Day, contrary to Law." An appeal to the legislature brought merely "leave to withdraw," but finally the Board of Aldermen granted them "liberty to place temporary bars in School street, and Common street, near to the Church . . . leaving sufficient space for a carriage to pass at a moderate foot-pace."

To step from the passing crowds of Tremont Street today

into the quiet and calm interior of King's Chapel is to enter the very atmosphere of one of Wren's old London churches. As we walk down the aisle and stop before the beautiful monument to Shirley's wife and daughter on the south wall, we seem to see the Governor and his accomplished lady, for so short a time to occupy that place. "Governors, Chief Justices, Judges; . . . English noblemen and gentlemen; officers of the Royal Army and Navy; . . . distinguished physicians, great merchants occupy the pews on either hand," to be followed later by Justices of the Supreme Court, Senators and Representatives in Congress, ministers of foreign courts, brilliant members of the bar, college presidents, men eminent in the arts and sciences. "On some winter's afternoon," said Dr. Greenwood, "as I have remained here after the congregation have retired, and sate, while the early darkness was falling . . . I could not resist the momentary impression that they were indeed the realities, and we the poor shadows, flitting shadowlike before them."

All about on the walls are memorials to notable members of the parish and congregation. On the north side is a marble tablet to that Charles Apthorp, merchant and liberal benefactor, who with his large family occupied the pew by the third pair of columns on the south aisle. His fourth son, East, we shall soon find as first rector of Christ Church in Cambridge. William Sullivan's monument is on the south wall. On the left in the vestibule as we enter is a modest tablet of green slate to the memory of the church's architect, Peter Harrison, and a memorial to another noted architect of more recent times—Robert Swain Peabody, son of one of the church's ministers, and a vestryman and warden—is on the wall at the right of the chancel. On the north side of the porch, in the churchyard, just inside the iron railing, there is a monument with a long inscription in French to the memory of the young Chevalier de St. Sauveur, "First Chamberlain of his Royall Highness Count d'Artois, brother of his Majesty the King of France." De St. Sauveur, a lieutenant on one of d'Estaing's ships in the harbor in 1778, met death in an attempt to quell a street riot. He was buried in the vaults beneath the Chapel.

In the tower of King's Chapel hangs Paul Revere's most famous bell, the largest that he and Joseph Warren Revere ever cast. It weighs over a ton. Much of the metal came from the older bell recast, the tradition being that silver added to the metal gives its especially beautiful tone. Once it was rung as the passing bell, to tell the town of a death—three times three for a man and three times two for a woman, with a stroke for each year of life. For over a hundred years Bostonians have known this bell. Its sound is so individual that it can be recognized far away, and still its voice goes out from the heart of the city to answer the singing voice of its sister of Christ's Church in the North End.

III

THE OLD NORTH AND SOME OTHER OLD BOSTON CHURCHES

OLDEST of Boston's churches now standing is the "Old North"— Christ Church in Salem Street in the North End. Probably most of its fame today is due to the hanging of the lanterns and the romantic tale of the "Ride," as related somewhat inaccurately by Longfellow. Yet architecturally, with its beautiful interior skillfully restored about thirty years ago, it is scarcely second to King's Chapel as an example of the English church plan. "Dr. Cutler's Church stands at the North End, the Royal Chapel at the centre; and I think another at the South will be highly necessary," wrote Thomas Harward to the Bishop of London in 1731.

The first record of Christ Church reads:

"Laus Deo: Boston, New England.

"The second day of September, 1722. At the request of several Gentlemen, who purchased a peice of Ground at the North End of Boston to build a church on, The Reverend Mr Samuel Myles ordered his Clerk to give Notice to his Congregation That all those who were willing to Contribute towards Erecting another Church at the North end of Boston were desired to meet at King's Chappel the Wednesday following.

"Agreeable to which Notification Severall Persons assembled, and chose Mr John Barnes Treasurer; Thomas Graves Esqr, Messrs George Cradock, Anthony Blount, John Gibbons, Thomas Selby, and George Monk a Committee to receive subscriptions and build a Church on Said Ground at the North end of Boston."

The list of two hundred and fourteen subscribers, many of whom were members of King's Chapel, was headed by the Right Honorable Thomas, Earl of Thanet, His Excellency Francis Nicholson, Esq., Governor of South Carolina, and Dr. Trapp, and the total amount subscribed was £2,184. 14s. The already low rate of exchange of the currency (Old Tenor) with English sterling was to fall lower and lower as the province continued to pay in paper currency for the "glories" of the French War.

Sad to relate, there seems to have been not a little jealousy and ill feeling among the older clergy in the colony who sought the place. Matthias Plant wrote from Newbury to Dr. Bearcroft:

"Mr. Mossom of Marblehead says there are but three Old England clergymen in these parts,—viz., Mr. Harris, myself, and you; and these fellows are going home for orders, and they will get the best places in the country and take the bread from off our trenchers . . . and we that have served the church must . . . take up with their leavings. We now who have stood the brunt of the battle and laid the foundation of the churches in this country, are not so much as consulted who shall be their minister. Mr. Harris is resolved to write to my Lord Bishop to oppose their ordination."

But on the 15th of April, 1723, Mr. Myles of King's Chapel laid the first stone of the foundation, with the words, doubtless considered highly appropriate, *"May the Gates of Hell never prevail against it!"*

The first rector was Timothy Cutler, one of the "fellows" who had gone home for orders. Cutler, who had been a Congregational minister at Stamford, Connecticut, was then rector (president) of Yale College. With two tutors and four other ministers he had "doubted the validity" (some were "fully persuaded of the invalidity") of presbyterian ordination. The trustees voted to "excuse the Rev. Mr. *Cutler* from all further Service as Rector of Yale College."

"It has caused some indignation," the trustees recorded, "to see the vile indignity cast by these *cudweeds* upon those excellent servants of God who were the leaders of the flock" and "to see the horrid character of more than one or two who have got themselves qualified with Episcopal Ordination, . . . disturbing the Churches of New England . . . in a town of several hundred families of Christians better than themselves."

Cutler and some of the others had "determined to declare themselves professors of the Church of England as soon as they shall understand they will be supported at home," and in November, 1722, he with Samuel Johnson and Daniel Brown sailed for England for ordination at the hands of the Bishop of London. Both Oxford and Cambridge conferred the degree of Doctor of Theology upon Cutler, and he returned to preach his first sermon in the newly completed church in December, 1723, beginning a rectorate of more than forty years. Johnson, born at Guilford, Connecticut, who had been minister of the Congregational Church at West Haven, has been called "the Father of Episcopacy in Connecticut." He became the first president of King's (Columbia) College. It is a curious fact that the grandson of this "father of Episcopacy" married the granddaughter of the great New England apostle of Calvinism, Jonathan Edwards.

With the opening of the new church there were the seemingly inevitable dissensions with departing members about their pews. In April, 1724, it was voted "that those Gentlemen who are already gone to the North Church shall have a consideration for their Pews, one half of the first cost. Also, that those Gentlemen who shall for the future go to the North Church shall have no consideration at all for their pews."

"At the first opening of my Church," Dr. Cutler wrote in 1727, "I had generally an audience of about 400 persons, which is now increased to about 700 or 800." Boston had now a population of from twenty to twenty-four thousand, and was "continually growing in Business and Riches."

As we have seen, about 1727 the colonies had been placed under the ecclesiastical jurisdiction of the see of London, and Bishop Gibson had appointed Roger Price as his "commissary," with authority to call conventions of the Episcopal clergy in New England. The first of these was held at Christ Church in September, 1738, when the vestry voted "That a handsome Dinner be provided for the s^d^ Rever^d^ Gent^n^ of the Clergy, and that the Wardens of Each Church and the Treasurer of the Charitable Society be invited." Some years later we find in the records:

"P^d^ one 1/3 p^t^ of the Charge of An Entertainment at ye Royal Exch^a^ Tavern last Easter, in Conjunction wth ye Wardens of Christ and Trinity Churches, made for ye Ministers at ye Convention. Am^o^ to £22. 10. 00—£7. 10. 00."

A note each year records the steady depreciation of the currency.

During Cutler's rectorate there was a long drawn-out controversy and much litigation in protest against the payment of "Rates in the Support of the Dissenting way of Worship." "Here," said Greenwood, "was consistency at least. Dissenters in England were and still are obliged to support the clergy of the Establishment, besides obliging themselves to support their own." In other words, what was sauce for the goose was sauce for the gander.

On his return from Georgia in 1736, Charles Wesley, then still within the fold of the Church of England, passed a month in Boston and preached in Christ Church and probably at King's Chapel. Whitefield came to Boston four years later, but although he attended service at King's Chapel and afterwards went home with Commissary Price, he received no invitation to preach at any of the Episcopal churches. He recorded in his diary that in the afternoon he preached to about four thousand in Dr. Colman's church, in Brattle Street. The bells were rung, "the streets filled with people, with coaches and chairs," wrote Dr. Cutler. "The Conventicles were crowded; but he chose rather our Common, where multitudes might see him in his awful postures; besides that in one crowded conventicle, before he came in, six were killed with fright." One more sad illustration "of the bitterness into which dislike could betray a Christian minister." According to Wesley's own account, "The meetinghouse [the New South] being filled, on a sudden all the people were in an uproar and so unaccountably surprised, that some threw themselves out of the windows, others . . . out of the gallery, and others trampled upon one another, so that five were actually killed. . . . I gave notice that I would immediately preach upon the Common. The weather was wet, but many thousands followed me."

March 6, 1749, the vestry book records:

"Whereas Mr Buck has Given Offence to ye Church by his Obstinate and irreverent Behavior in ye house of God, and suffering others So to Doo, and likewise his not performing to ye Satisfaction of ye Church As an Organist,

"Therefore its *Voted,* that the Church has no more service for him as an Organist, he being not Worthy of that Station."

Perhaps it was not without reason that Thomas Brattle had stipulated that his organist should be a "Sober person"; yet Buck may have had cause for not performing "to ye Satisfaction," for three years later the vestry voted "That Mr. Thos Johnson Make for the Church . . . a *New Organ* with the Echo Equall to That of Trinity Church of this Town." Thomas Johnson was an escutcheon maker who built the first organ of American manufacture used in Boston.

Evidently there was rivalry as to organs about this time, for King's Chapel got its new one four years later.

The North End sexton, like his brother at King's Chapel, had to contend with the "Unlucky Boyes" (as his successor no doubt does today, though perhaps for other reasons). On November 21, 1726, the vestry voted "That for the future the Sexton shall keep ye rails at the Altar clear from Boys and Negroes setting there." And also "That no Nailes nor pinns be put in the pillars nor the front of the Gallerys with a design to hang Hatts on."

In the Vestry Book for 1746 is the record:

"Whereas Oners of the 2 [?]Prevetrs Queen of Hungary hath made a present to Christ Church in Boston, of 4 Cherubims and 2 Glass Branches Taken by ye Said Vessell.

"Voted, That the Branches be hung in ye body of the Church. And ye Cherubims placed on ye Top of the Organ."

The following remarkable event, recorded in the "Newsletter" of September 8–15, 1757, may well be quoted in full:

"Tuesday in the Afternoon, John Childs, who had given public Notice of his Intention to Fly from the Steeple of Dr. Cutler's Church, perform'd it to the Satisfaction of a great Number of Spectators; and yesterday in the Afternoon he again perform'd it twice. The last Time he set off with two Pistols loaded, one of which he discharged in his Descent; the other missing fire, he cock'd and snap'd again before he reached the Place prepared to receive him. It is suppos'd from the Steeple to the Place where the Rope was fix'd was about 700 Feet upon a Slope, and that he was about 16 or 18 Seconds performing it each Time. As these Performances led many People from their Business, he is forbid flying any more in the Town. The said Child says he has flown from the highest Steeples in England, and off the Monument, by the Duke of Cumberland's Desire."

Seemingly ever self-assertive and quarrelsome in religious matters, these early New Englanders were incorrigible killjoys.

In August, 1765, Dr. Cutler, the "stately rector" of Christ

CHRIST CHURCH (OLD NORTH, 1723) *Boston, Massachusetts*

Church, then in his eighty-third year, passed to his reward. Long disabled by paralysis, for years he had been incapacitated for his sacred functions.

The church's second rector, Dr. Mather Byles, like his predecessor, was a former Congregationalist and came from Connecticut, where he had had a church at New London. His father, Mather Byles, Sr., a grandson of Increase Mather, was pastor of the Hollis Street Church, a correspondent of Alexander Pope, and something of a punster and a wit. What would the two old Puritans have thought of one of the family in the hated English Church!

In May, 1768, Mather Byles, Jr., went to England for ordination, returning to Boston for his charge at Christ Church the following September. But momentous events were on the way. Between the time when they had heard their last King proclaimed by trumpet from the Old Town House balcony and the day when the streets echoed to the retreating drums of the British, there were to be unhappy years for the clergy and many of the people of the Church of England in Boston.

Although Dr. Caner wrote from Halifax in May, 1776, that Byles was among those who sought refuge there during the British evacuation, church documents state that he resigned in April, 1775, and "accepted an invitation from the church in Portsmouth, New Hampshire." At any rate we hear nothing of him on that fateful evening of April 18th, when Paul Revere's plans were so carefully made.

Christ Church steeple rose above all the landmarks in the town. Just across the street in his mother's house, lived Joseph Newman, the sexton, and brother of the organist. Unfortunately the house was full of British officers who were billeted there. Paul Revere as a boy had been one of the bell ringers at Christ's, and sometimes he went to church there. "About ten o'clock," he wrote afterwards, "Dr. Warren sent in great haste for me, and begged that I would immediately set off for Lexington, where Messrs. Hancock and Adams were, and acquaint them of the movement, and that it was thought they were the objects." Revere found Newman, who to avoid the officers, had got out of an upper story window, down over a roof, and was waiting in the street for orders. John Pulling, one of the vestrymen, went with him, and together they climbed to the belfry, Longfellow says:

"And lo! as he looks, on the belfry's height
A glimmer, and then a gleam of light!
He springs to the saddle, the bridle he turns."

Actually, however, when Colonel Conant and the other men in Charlestown saw the light Revere was still in Boston. It was about eleven o'clock when Bentley the boatbuilder and Thomas Richardson rowed him past the *Somerset* man-of-war to the Charlestown shore and he started on his ride.

The church was closed until August, 1778, when it was opened with Stephen Lewis, a chaplain in Burgoyne's army, as rector. Lewis was followed by William Montague, during whose rectorate, in 1789, the parish like others after the Revolution, was incorporated under an act of the General Court.

The North End, now largely given over to an Italian American and Jewish population, once was the "court" end of Boston. Here, in near-by North Square and the adjacent streets, dwelt the Clarks and the Rowes, the Hutchinsons and the Franklands. Sir Harry Frankland had bought the Clark house, and here in 1775 Lady Frankland came from her home in Hopkinton, to which she had returned after her husband's death in England. For the journey from Hopkinton she had a guard of six soldiers; and she reached Boston in time to watch the Battle of Bunker Hill from the upper windows.

Christ Church is said to have been built from a design by William Price, a rather notable character. In early life he was a cabinetmaker, but in 1770 he was described as a "Picterman"—a dealer in books and engravings; and his business must have been remarkably profitable for the times. We are much indebted to him for an early map and views of the town. A zealous churchman, he held a pew in each of the three Episcopal churches. He contributed largely towards the fund for building Trinity Church and also to the rebuilding of King's Chapel, which he attended until his death, at the age of eighty-seven. He left to the Chapel the William Price fund, the cause of much later contention and litigation.

Price contributed towards the erection of Christ Church, was one of its first vestrymen and later warden, and for a year acted as organist without "Sallery."

The present spire, which replaces the one blown down in the

INTERIOR OF CHRIST CHURCH *Boston, Massachusetts*

THE PARK STREET CHURCH (1809) *Boston, Massachusetts*

September gale of 1804, was built from a design by Charles Bulfinch. It is similar to the old spire, though Bulfinch made slight changes in proportions and details. The original spire was built in a near-by pasture and hoisted into place. In 1847 the present one was repaired in the same way.

About thirty-five years ago the ownership of the church had fallen to eight pew holders, and these agreed to place control in the hands of Bishop Lawrence. Funds were generously subscribed, as usual with anything which the Bishop undertook, and the work had the interest and cooperation of two Boston architects especially fitted for the work.

The exterior paint was removed, restoring the brickwork to its original condition, the chancel deepened, and the walls replaced in their early position with the large window which had been plastered over. The wooden vestry, a bad fire hazard, was rebuilt of brick, and recently the small house on the south side facing the yard has been torn down.

The original pulpit had been given to a church at Otis, Massachusetts. That of Trinity Church, Newport, of the same period, was used as a model, and the sounding board hung by its rod from the hole in the oak beam above the ceiling from which the old sounding board had been hung. The box pews with their center aisle were restored as nearly as possible to their original condition; sixty-five of them with plates bearing the names of their first owners. The bust of Washington at one side of the chancel was presented by Shubael Bell, senior warden, in 1815. Lafayette, when he saw it, is reported to have said, "Yes, that is the man I knew, and more like him than any other portrait." It is believed to have been the first memorial to Washington in any public place. The fine old chandeliers are the "branches" captured from the French ship by the privateersman during the French and Indian War of 1746, as were the statuettes, ("cherubims"), on either side of the organ—intended for a Canadian convent. The interior of the church, with that persistent determination to attribute everything of the period to the influence of Wren, is described as "in a marked degree a reproduction of St. James's Piccadilly."

Although the First and Old South meetinghouses as well as King's Chapel had a special pew for the governor, Christ Church never had one. In 1727 it was "*Voted,* That a Pew be expeditiously built next the Pulpit and lin'd handsomely for the use of the Gentlemen of ye Bay of Handoras who have been or shall be Benefactors of this Church," thus wisely encouraging future patronage from gentlemen who had invested wisely and well in the lands to the south, while expressing due gratitude for benefits received. The gentlemen of "Handoras" had presented to the church a valuable cargo of logwood.

The full peal of eight bells still hangs in the tower. "We are the first ring of bells cast for the British Empire in North America —A. R. Ano 1744," says one. Which tells us that they were made by Abel Rudhall of Gloucester in England, "who cast us all." "God preserve the Church of England," is on another. One of them was given by Governor Shirley. The largest weighs 1,545 pounds.

Perhaps the fact that as a boy Paul Revere had helped to ring this peal may have accounted for his lifelong interest in bells and for his making them later. Those from his foundry compared favorably with the English bells; but he never quite equaled the tone of the best, such as those of Christ Church, because, it was said, of the peculiar quality of the more elastic copper, no longer to be obtained.

And so, as we hear the bell in the King's Chapel answering its sister in the North End, we think of the young Revere, who once pulled on a rope in the tower, and grew up to make the bell for the old stone chapel in the heart of the city.

East of Christ Church is the recently completed Paul Revere Mall, extending to Hanover Street. Here is Cyrus Dallin's equestrian statue of Paul Revere, and opposite, closing the vista, Bulfinch's church in Hanover Street, now the Roman Catholic Church of St. Stephen. The construction of the Mall has opened up a charming view of the apse and spire of the Old North entirely new to the present generation; a view for many years obstructed by the old houses in the rear. Here along the Mall on any pleasant day may be discovered a true outdoor scene from Italy. On the benches and crowding about the long tables provided for their comfort, hundreds of happy Italian Americans play their games while their women bask in the sun and gossip with their neighbors, and their children romp and shout to their hearts' content, away from the traffic of the crowded streets. An inscription around the great stone basin of the fountain in the center tells us that it

OLD WEST CHURCH (1806) *Boston, Massachusetts*

CHARLES STREET CHURCH (1807) *Boston, Massachusetts*

is to George Robert White and his bequest that the people of the city are indebted for this benefaction.

At least four other old Boston churches should be mentioned. Best known probably is the Park Street Church, designed by Peter Banner and built in 1809. It is particularly notable for its fine spire. Unfortunately the interior has been much spoiled by injudicious alterations. The old West Church in Cambridge Street, now a branch library, was built in 1806 from designs by Asher Benjamin and probably is the best remaining example of his work, though the treatment of the tower and front is far from graceful. The highly ornamented galleries still remain, and originally the interior must have been of considerable interest. The Charles Street Meetinghouse, of very similar design, also was built from Benjamin's drawings. The interior has been greatly changed, but after a life of many vicissitudes it was finally saved from destruction by the subscriptions of a group of interested people in the neighborhood and is now held in trust to be used as a sort of community center.

Still standing deserted in the midst of its old churchyard in South Boston is St. Augustine's, a quaint little red brick building dating from the latter part of the eighteenth century, in the time of Bishop Cheverus. That well beloved first Roman Catholic Bishop of Boston, friend of Unitarian James Freeman, for his courtly manners, kindly ways, and broad-minded common sense was welcomed into the exclusive intellectual and aristocratic coterie which graced Boston society of the early years of the nineteenth century.

IV

CHRIST CHURCH, CAMBRIDGE, THE "OLD SHIP," AND THE ELIOT CHURCH AT NATICK

ANY OR ALL accounts of Christ Church, Cambridge, seem naturally to begin with East Apthorp, for though Dr. Caner of King's Chapel wrote the original letter to Dr. Bearcroft, the secretary of the Society for the Propagation of the Gospel in Foreign Parts, appealing for funds for a church in Cambridge, it was Apthorp, the first rector, who contributed his salary for the two years and a half until the church was built, and who in addition bore the brunt of the criticism and abuse from the people of the churches of Boston and vicinity strenuously objecting to any further addition to the strength of the hated Church of England.

The Reverend East Apthorp was a son of the great Boston merchant, Charles Apthorp and his wife Grizel, whom we saw walking with their eighteen children down the aisle to their pew in King's Chapel. East was born in Brighton, went to the Boston Latin School and finished his education at Cambridge in England, where he was ordained and made a fellow of Jesus College. On his father's death in 1758 he returned to Boston and married Elizabeth Hutchinson, sister of the governor. The next year he received his appointment as missionary from the Society for the Propagation of the Gospel and settled in Cambridge.

"A cultivated and scholarly man," he obtained a gift of a hundred pounds from the Society, when the Harvard College library was burnt, towards its replacement. In Cambridge he built the finest house in town, still standing on Plympton Street and still sometimes known as the "Bishop's Palace." It is now the residence of the master of Adams House. The old house has had a long and varied history, being occupied at various times by Borlands, Plymptons, and Bulfinches and their descendants.

When, in 1761, sufficient funds had been subscribed to ensure the building of the church, the architect naturally was Peter Harrison, the architect of King's Chapel.

Accounts differ as to when Harrison came to America. It has repeatedly been said that he and Smibert the painter came over with Bishop Berkeley to Newport; but Samuel F. Batchelder, who wrote a history of Christ Church and a sketch of Harrison's life, says that there is no authentic evidence of his being in Newport before 1740, when he came "a passenger with Captain Patterson." His brother Joseph arrived about the same time. It is generally believed that they came of an aristocratic Yorkshire family, and had had architectural training, and there is a tradition that Peter was an assistant to Vanbrugh in building the Duke of Marlborough's great pile, Blenheim Palace. His first work in America, however, seems to have been making several important surveys and maps for the colonial government. Both brothers settled down at Newport, where we shall find them in another chapter.

In 1766 Harrison succeeded his brother as collector of customs at New Haven, which brought him into trouble when the Revolution broke out. A mob looted his house and destroyed his library and drawings, and this well may have shortened his life, for he died in 1775. Smibert's rather stiff portrait shows him as an aristocratic, thin-lipped young man looking down his long thin nose, with a high forehead sloping back to a powdered wig.

With all of Batchelder's praise for Harrison's design of the Cambridge church we cannot entirely agree. "A reduced and simplified replica of King's Chapel," it scarcely is; "in wood instead of stone, though with all the 'feeling' of stone in its proportions and details"—exactly what it should not be, and the very fault which the native designers and builders so wisely and cleverly avoided. He then goes on to tell us that, "had the parish funds ever permitted carrying out the original intention of finishing the exterior in roughcast," the effect of stone would have been intensified. But the side elevations with their many-lighted, round-headed windows and the detail of the frieze and cornice are quite charming, though, as in the case of King's Chapel, we could wish that the tower with its rather severe and commonplace belfry could have been completed with an adequate spire, to add much of external grace and elegance.

Except for the enlargement by adding two bays between the

chancel and the nave in 1857, the exterior is practically unchanged. When these alterations were made it was found that the timbers had been joined at the proper point of separation, the archtect evidently having foreseen a probable enlargement.

In one important feature the interior is a decided improvement over that of King's Chapel. There are no side galleries, that doubtless necessary effort at economy which has spoiled the interior effect of most of our early meetinghouses and churches. The coved plaster vault over the nave springs from the "returned" entablatures above the capitals of the Ionic columns—a favorite motif, but always rather artificial and unconvincing. The aisle ceilings are flat. Smaller columns without pedestals support the old organ loft over the entrance.

Various changes have been made in the interior during the past hundred years, all of the more recent ones with the aim of restoring the church as nearly as possible to its original condition. When alterations or additions have been made it has been with the greatest care to conform to the style and character of the original structure.

The original high "wineglass" pulpit faced the center aisle, with stairs at the back, much like the old pulpit which may still be seen in Trinity Church in Newport. In 1853 the forty-four high box pews were removed and replaced by more modern slip pews. During the 1880's the church was "decorated" in accordance with prevailing Victorian taste. Although this was as far as possible from the character of the Colonial or Georgian work of the period when the church was built, it was fairly good of its kind, and to describe it as "hideous" is perhaps not quite true. About the same time the chancel was extended to make room for the vested choir of men and boys, which was moved from the gallery.

The church has had no fewer than five organs. In 1845 the fine old English organ which had been damaged during the Revolution was replaced. The new one was used until 1860, when a third was installed. About 1876 this was removed from the loft or gallery over the door and placed so as to serve both the church and the "chapel." A year or two later it was succeeded by a fourth. In 1941 the present very fine organ with most modern electrical manual and other appliances was installed as a memorial to Sarah Moody Cushing Toppan. The interior of the church has recently

CHRIST CHURCH (1761) *Cambridge, Massachusetts*
Designed by Peter Harrison

INTERIOR OF CHRIST CHURCH *Cambridge, Massachusetts*

been painted the light gray appropriate to work of the period. The new choir and sanctuary stalls, and new pulpit and reading desk, are in keeping with other work of the time when the church was built. The fine crystal chandeliers are the gift of Francis B. Sayre in memory of his wife, a daughter of President Wilson. The pulpit and choir stalls are also memorials. A large and adequate parish house is soon to be built, for which funds have been raised and plans drawn.

The cornerstone of the church was laid in 1760—an impressive ceremony in which the governor, Sir Francis Bernard, took part, and on the 15th of October of the next year the first service was held in the new building. The young rector preached to an aristocratic congregation, the gentlemen in satin knee breeches with white silk stockings and laced coats and their ladies in looped-up skirts of flowered silks and high-heeled slippers. Among them, it is said, was a liberal sprinkling from the dissenting churches of Cambridge, who had come out of curiosity to witness the popish ceremonies of the opening of this unwelcome addition to the strength of their Church of England neighbors.

This was the time of the long drawn-out and heated battle of the pamphleteers known as the Mayhew Controversy: "Whether the Society *for the propagation of the Gospel in Foreign parts* conform to the design of their incorporation, by maintaining episcopal churches in the settled Towns and Villages of *North America*: or whether they have not misapplied a fund originally *limited* to the conversion of the Heathens."

As a matter of fact, in the beginning they did "conform to the design of their incorporation," for the preamble of their charter granted in 1701 called for the (1) "Maintenance of an orthodox clergy in the plantations, colonies, and factories of Great Britain beyond the seas, for the instruction of the King's loving subjects in the Christian religion: (2) other provisions necessary for the propagation of the Gospel in those parts . . ." Ten years later, possibly because of the rumpus stirred up in New England, with the feeling "that the conversion of the heathen should be given more emphasis," resolutions were carried stating "That the design of propagating the gospel in foreign parts does chiefly and principally relate to the conversion of heathens and infidels, and therefore that branch of it ought to be prosecuted preferably to all others." The arrival of four Indian sachems in London provided an added stimulus, and Queen Anne gave £400 for a mission post and chapel to be built in their country.

Jonathan Mayhew, a graduate of Harvard College, was pastor of the West Church in Boston. In a number of published pamphlets he pressed all the old arguments against Episcopacy and the Established Church, and particularly the claim that the funds of the S.P.G. had been "shamefully perverted," and that from their charter and from "the early sermons preached before it in London, the heathen were the primary objects of its care, and were now wholly neglected, while the Society in twenty-five years had expended £35,000 on its missions"—meaning in the establishment of churches in the settled towns and villages of the colonies, as at Cambridge and Marblehead, rather than in sending missionaries into the wilderness to convert the Indians.

The controversy as to the use of the funds of the Society, however, was only one episode in the agitation. Stirred by the efforts of the Episcopalians to establish churches and obtain an American bishop, Mayhew and others had preached and published pamphlet after pamphlet, only to be pursued by corresponding attacks from the opposite side. As might be expected from what we know of the prevailing vindictive manners and habits of the contestants on both sides, many of the retorts were purely personal. "There has been one pop after another at me," Mayhew wrote; but "they have not taken a right aim. Most of them, indeed have discharged little besides mud and dirt at me." Mr. Edes, in completing the second volume of the "Annals of King's Chapel," devotes nearly forty pages to this controversy—throughout, a sordid and ill-natured dispute between the two factions.

For several years the conflict raged in New England with caustic comment and sarcasm on both sides, characteristic of the times. John Aplin, a Providence lawyer, wrote: "I had rather be an inspired Ass in the Service of my Maker, than an Apostate Priest in the Pay of his Adversary. As to the Fathers, I shall take leave to say, They were most of them Reverend Old Dotards." The Lord Brethren were still "inspired," the Churchmen "Apostates" and "Dotards."

Unfortunately the ardent and well-meaning young rector of Christ Church became involved in the controversy. Though described as a "most mild and Christian gentleman" who "suffered very keenly during this controversy" and was "actuated by the best motives," he took the leading part against Mayhew. Tired of constant wrangling and criticism, in 1765, Apthorp returned to England where Archbishop Secker apppointed him to the rectory of Croydon. Here he remained for twenty-eight years, evidently much liked by his parishioners, for when, about 1790, he lost his sight, they made him a gift of £2000. About 1778 he was given in addition to Croydon the rectory of St. Mary-le-Bow. Well educated, of agreeable manners and good breeding and perhaps not without the influence of desirable family connections, he received one preferment after another. In 1790 he was made a prebendary of St. Paul's with the offer of the Bishopric of Kildare in Ireland, which he declined on account of ill health. In 1793 he was given the valuable prebend of Finsbury, attached to St. Paul's, obliging him to resign his other livings. In 1782 he had lost his first wife, five years later marrying a daughter of John Crich, a Suffolk squire. He lived to be eighty-four, dying in 1816 at Cambridge, England, where he was buried in the chapel of Jesus College, of which he was a graduate.

Such was East Apthorp, who, as a young man of twenty-six, became the first rector of Christ Church.

For two or three years the church had no settled rector; but in 1767 Winwood Sergeant came to Cambridge for eight peaceful and apparently prosperous years. The outbreak of the Revolution brought trouble to the rector of Christ Church as it did to most of the other Church of England clergy. The Tory aristocracy were leaving Cambridge. Only the lieutenant governor, Thomas Oliver, who lived at Elmwood, stayed on until a mob gathered in front of his house to force his resignation. Sergeant went first to Kingston, New Hampshire, and from there to Newbury. "I have lost not less than £300 in household furniture and books destroyed and pillaged" he wrote. A Connecticut regiment was quartered in the church, organ pipes were melted into bullets and the colonial troops committed other acts of sacrilege.

Washington had arrived in Cambridge in July, 1775. Sufficient repairs were made to fit the church for use, and on New Year's Eve he attended when Colonel William Palfrey read the service, using a form of prayer which he had written in place of that in the Prayer Book for the King and royal family. Mrs. Washington and Mrs. Custis were in the church.

After Burgoyne's surrender, when the captured Hessian and British troops were quartered in Cambridge, an unfortunate incident occurred which resulted in the greatest damage to the church. Evidently some of the officers were allowed more or less freedom. A young English lieutenant, Richard Brown, was driving down Prospect Hill in Somerville and lost control of his horses. A raw and inexperienced guard posted at the foot of the hill challenged him, and shot him dead when he could not stop his horses. Obviously the incident was deeply regretted by the American officers. The funeral, with all military honors, was held in Christ Church. According to tradition the coffin was placed in the Vassall vault, and during the burial service in the crypt vandals ransacked and defaced the church, destroying the pulpit and reading desk and communion table, breaking the pipes of the organ and damaging the bellows. The building was now almost completely wrecked, and the congregation scattered. For a dozen years the church was closed and neglected, and it was not until 1790 that it was sufficiently repaired for services once more, when Dr. Parker of Trinity Church, Boston, preached from the text "Now therefore ye are no more strangers and foreigners, but fellowcitizens with the saints, and of the household of God." It was another thirty years, however, before a committee appointed by the diocese obtained subscriptions totaling three thousand dollars for the thorough repair of the building, three hundred of which was given by Harvard students. A number of changes in the interior were made at this time. For fifteen years more the church was served by various rectors, until in 1839 Dr. Nicholas Hoppin began a long and successful rectorship of thirty-five years. During this time the building was enlarged, and in October, 1861, the hundredth anniversary was celebrated with an impressive ceremony, when the peal of thirteen bells given by Harvard graduates and alumni was rung for the first time.

In the vestry is the sword of Barlow Trecothick, Lord Mayor of London at the time the church was built, through whose efforts the first organ was obtained. He married Apthorp's eldest sister. A younger sister married Thomas Bulfinch, father of the architect. The church has the communion plate given to King's Chapel by

William and Mary in 1694 which Governor Hutchinson transferred to Christ Church, folio Prayer Books with the prayers for the King struck out, and other old books of interest.

From the time of Dr. Hoppin to the present, the church has had a succession of distinguished rectors. In 1931 the congregation of St. John's Chapel of the Episcopal Theological School joined with the parish. Relations between the two had always been intimate, and deans of the school frequently preached at Christ Church.

In the old burying ground, dating from 1635 or earlier, between Christ Church and the church of the First Parish, lie the earliest settlers of Cambridge and some of the most noted and distinguished of the colony: a royal governor, judges, presidents of Harvard; men of learning and of wealth. Here lie the college's first president, Henry Dunster and seven other early presidents. Here in a tomb near the entrance by the First Parish Church was buried Governor Jonathan Belcher, and in the Trowbridge tomb near it, the painter, Washington Allston. The Vassall tomb is near here too; a freestone slab on five fluted square columns. Among the early stones is that of Major Daniel Geokin, with Eliot, a constant friend and protector of the Indians; and long unmarked, Samuel Green who began the printing of Eliot's Indian Bible, and that first printer in the colony, Stephen Daye. Here are the schoolmaster Elijah Corlett and Gregory Stone, ancestor of the innumerable progeny of Stones, whose son built the first house in Framingham.

Several young students of the college are buried here, among them Noah Merrick, drowned in the river in 1762, and Charles Cutter, "Lacu Cantabrigiensi casu submersi," seventeen years later. Cutter was a son of Dr. Ammi Ruhamah Cutter of New Hampshire.

In the large slab tomb near the entrance was buried John Stedman, who crossed the ocean with the family of the Reverend Jesse Glover, who died on the voyage. Stedman became a successful merchant in Cambridge, was selectman for sixty years, served as ensign in the militia, and filled a long term as county treasurer. His daughters all married well known and distinguished men, one having four husbands before her father died, at the age of ninety-two.

Unique among all the old meetinghouses and churches of Massachusetts is the First Parish Meetinghouse, commonly called the "Old Ship," at Hingham.

The Old Ship is the oldest church building in New England; the oldest wooden one and the oldest in continual use in the United States. Architecturally it stands alone, the one example of this primitive type which has been restored to its original condition. With the exception of the early eighteenth century gallery additions, thanks to careful restorations of 1930 we see it today much as it was originally built; and it is just as it was twenty years before the Revolution.

Hingham in many ways is still the most charming of the smaller seacoast towns of Massachusetts. Though it has felt to some extent the encroachment of the great shipping industries of near-by Quincy, fine seventeenth and eighteenth century houses still line the elm-shaded streets. A number of these are the summer homes of Boston people, though most of them are occupied by all-the-year-round residents.

The Old Ship, the second meetinghouse built by the First Parish in Hingham, stands on the slope of the hill above Main Street. Reasons for the name would seem to be sufficiently obvious. It was built by ship carpenters, and the heavy knees and other curved timbers of the roof certainly suggest the frame of an old wooden ship. Trees were felled near by, by members of the parish, and in addition some of the timbers in the first little building were used in the new one.

The original structure was built in 1681. In 1730 the extension for the west gallery was made, and in 1755 that on the opposite side. It was at this time that the remarkable high pulpit and the first box pews were built, in place of the crude wooden benches used for the first seventy-five years. We suppose it was for use on this pulpit that the "red velvet pulpit-cuchion and case" were obtained from the "New Brick" meetinghouse (the "Cockerel") in Boston, in exchange for six cords of wood during the hard winter of 1779.

In 1731 a plaster ceiling was put in below the heavy crossbeams of the trusses, which remained until the restoration of the building in 1930. In 1791 the old meetinghouse narrowly escaped destruction. It had been voted to build a new one; but the vote

THE OLD SHIP (1681) *Hingham, Massachusetts*

was reconsidered, alterations were made two years later, and the old church was saved. In 1869 came all the calamities of the Victorian age—never, perhaps, more incongruous than they were in the Old Ship at Hingham. The old box pews were torn out, and curving pews installed. The beautiful old high pulpit was taken down, though the old sounding board was left in place; and a carpet was laid on the floor and the platform steps. But it became the desire of the people of Hingham and of others interested in our early architecture to see the old meetinghouse carefully restored, and in 1930, through the generosity of Eben Howard Gay, a descendant of the third minister, this was at last accomplished. Full credit for this should be given to the architects, Messrs. Smith and Walker of Boston, whose work has been most skillfully done. Fortunately the original pulpit with its beautiful panelwork had not been destroyed. This is thought to have been modeled after the pulpit in the church at Cohasset. The compass ornament on the sounding board suggests the influence of the shipbuilders. Parts of some of the old pews were used in their restoration. It was discovered that many of the doors and other woodwork had been preserved and were still in the possession of descendants of the original owners. Advertising actually brought back thirty-two of the eighty doors, which have been hung in their original locations in accordance with an old plan and descriptions. The finish of the new woodwork—a task requiring particular skill—has been remarkably well done, and although it is practically impossible to reproduce exactly the patina of age and long years of use, probably only the most experienced in such work could tell the parts which are actually old from the new.

The Old Ship has always had a bell, and the present one, the fifth, has hung in the "turret" since 1822. It has been rung every Sunday morning for six score years and more; and on the death of every President since Abraham Lincoln it has tolled.

Particular mention should be made of the Old Ship's sexton and custodian, Frank W. Reed, to whose unfailing patience, kindness and courtesy, and intelligent interest and knowledge of all that concerns the old building every visitor is indebted. Akin to the best of sextons and vergers of the English parish churches and cathedrals, he and his two predecessors together have served the Old Ship for a hundred years. Would that there were more like him in our New England churches.

On the hill behind the church is the old burying ground with the graves of the early settlers. Remains of the fort built for protection against the Indians are still to be seen here.

At the side near the entrance to the burying ground is the memorial tower erected on the two hundred and seventy-fifth anniversary of the founding of the town. In the second story of this is a room dedicated to the memory of Peter Hobart, founder of the town and its first minister. This has been fitted up in the style of the time, and here are interesting relics and memorials of the early settlers. In the belfry above is a ring of eleven bells cast in England.

The first English visitor to Hingham as far as is known was Captain John Smith. After taking part in the Jamestown settlement he had returned to England; and in 1614—six years before the settlement at Plymouth—he was chosen by a company of London merchants to head an expedition to New England. Reaching land with his ships near Monhegan Island, on the Maine coast, he followed the shore southward with eight men in a small boat and entered Cohasset harbor.

The first settlement within the bounds of the present town was in 1633. Two years later a larger party came, led by the church's first minister, the Reverend Peter Hobart—most of them from old Hingham in English Norfolk. These had landed at Charlestown and coming down the harbor in an open pinnace into the small stream that runs through the town, started their settlement near the foot of Ship Street. The same year their first little meetinghouse was built on the slope of Main Street nearly opposite Derby Academy.

Five ministers served the church for almost two centuries and a half, an average of nearly fifty years—Dr. Ebenezer Gay and Joseph Richardson, the third and fifth, for sixty-nine and sixty-five years. From Peter Hobart, the first, was descended the sixth in line, the Reverend Calvin Lincoln. General Benjamin Lincoln, who received Cornwallis's sword at Yorktown, during much of his life attended church at the Old Ship, as did Abraham Lincoln's ancestor Samuel, who came to Hingham in 1637. Their pews are marked by tablets. General Lincoln became collector of the port of Boston. At this time the wife and daughter of the Reverend John Troutbeck occupied his house. Troutbeck had been missionary of the Society for the Propagation of the Gospel at Hopkinton, and later rector of King's Chapel. Two of Samuel Lincoln's descendants have been historians of Hingham—father and grandfather of the present representative of the family, who occupies the fine old house nearly opposite the church. There have always been Lincolns in Hingham. The old Garrison House on North Street has been occupied by nine generations of them. Thomas, the first to come, was a Norfolk weaver who arrived in 1633, two years before Hobart and his party.

The second minister was John Norton, who had a pastorate of thirty-eight years. His successor was Dr. Ebenezer Gay, known as the first American Unitarian, though Foote makes no reference to him in the "Annals of King's Chapel." Of forceful personality and pronounced religious views, the Doctor apparently was something of a wit. There is a story that a friend and he, riding to Boston, passed the gallows which stood on Roxbury Neck. His companion asked jocosely, "Where would you be, my friend, if those gallows had their due?" "Riding alone to Boston," was the prompt reply. Gay's successor at Hingham, Henry Ware, was called from the pulpit of the Old Ship to become Hollis Professor of Divinity at Harvard, so that the church is intimately connected with the Unitarian movement in New England.

Here is a church which seems to have avoided arguments over sites and rebuilding and has occupied the same structure for more than two hundred and sixty years—a short time for the age-old masonry buildings of Europe, but a remarkably long one under the fast-changing conditions of our own land.

One of the most charming small early nineteenth century meetinghouses in Massachusetts is the little Eliot Church in South Natick, built in 1828. Though the exterior is not elaborate, the tower with its arched belfry and balustraded clock stage and corner urns, the whole surmounted by a lantern and vane, and the Palladian window and recessed doorway below, are all entirely pleasing in their simplicity.

The interior is equally satisfactory, for any alterations that have been made are in keeping with the original work. Stairs on each side lead to the little white pulpit under an arch over the raised platform; and behind it is a corresponding arched motif on the wall, hung with a crimson drapery—the whole rarely attractive and pleasing from an architectural point of view, yet in every way fulfilling the requirements of a nonliturgical service. The arms and backs of the white slip pews are finished with light walnut, and there are red cushions on the seats and a red carpet on the aisles. The seating is arranged with the always desirable center aisle, discarded for reasons of economy in the remodeling of so many old churches. Nicely designed stairways on each side lead to the little gallery over the entrance for the organ and choir. Here is the only unsatisfactory feature of the interior; the ceiling is so low over the gallery that the tops of the organ pipes disappear into the space above.

On the wall under the gallery is a bronze tablet in memory of notable members of the church; among them John Perry of Roxbury "who came in the ship with John Eliot." He was Eliot's cousin and a member of his church in Roxbury. Here also are Samuel Perry who served in the Indian War and at Lexington; Amos Perry, magistrate and captain in the Continental army; John Jones of Dedham, magistrate under King George and a colonel of militia, and John Jones 2nd, of Princetown, a captain in the Revolutionary army.

Although this building, erected in 1828, is said to be on or very near the site of the first Indian church established by John Eliot in 1651, Bacon wrote nearly a hundred years ago in his history of the town: "The society worshipping in it are not understood as making any pretension to being the successors of the 'Praying Indian' church of 1650." The inscriptions by the door and on the walls inside would seem to indicate such a claim, however. Although it is described merely as the "Eliot Unitarian Church," four earlier churches with dates and the names of their preachers are described as "The First Indian Church—1651–1690," "The Second Indian Church—1700–1721," "The Third Meeting House," and "The Fourth Meeting House."

On the tablets, with the names of Eliot's successors, we find those of the Indian Daniel Takawambpait and the Indians' constant friend and protector, Daniel Gookin. Among other ministers of the present church in the nineteenth century was Horatio

ELIOT CHURCH (1828) *South Natick, Massachusetts*

Alger, father of the well known writer of moral thrillers and tales of adventure for boys before the days of movie Westerns and city bandits.

In the autumn of 1631, Eliot, a young man of twenty-seven, had come to Boston from Essex, in England, where he was born and where he had been an usher in a school kept by the Reverend Thomas Hooker.

Eliot became pastor of the church in Roxbury, and when, in 1646, the General Court of Massachusetts passed an act "to encourage attempts" to convert the Indians to Christianity, he began his life work as missionary. While he was searching for a place to establish a community, some of the Indians suggested a spot on the Charles River where is now the village of South Natick. In exchange for Indian lands at Deerfield, with the sanction of the General Court, the adjoining town of Dedham transferred a tract of six thousand acres to the Indians—to whom it probably rightfully belonged anyway. Here they built themselves some rude houses. One more substantial than the others was used as a church, and on this spot, in 1651, Natick was settled.

Eliot's Indians formed a self-governing community, ruled "by Mr. Eliot's advice" by the Mosaic Code. As such it continued until 1762, when by an act of the General Court Natick was "erected" into an English town, and the ever unfortunate Indians were placed under guardianship. In the French and Indian wars the New England tribes were pretty thoroughly subdued, but at the time of King Philip's uprising it had been seriously proposed in the General Court to build a wall eight feet high from the Charles River to Concord—one more demonstration, one would say, of the authorities' complete lack of understanding of the ways and habits of the Indians. It is said that of the more than four thousand who listened to Eliot's teaching, not one took part in King Philip's War.

"Since the death of Paul," said Edward Everett, "a nobler, truer, and warmer spirit than John Eliot never lived. . . . The history of the Christian Church does not contain an example of resolute, untiring, successful labor, superior to that of translating the entire Scriptures into the language of the native tribes of Massachusetts."

In addition to translating both the Old and New Testament,

Eliot prepared an Indian grammar. It is said that when the first Greek translation of the Bible was made seventy-two rabbis were employed to do the work; that at least that number of Christian students were engaged upon the Latin version before Jerome prepared the Vulgate text, and no fewer than fifty profound scholars combined to produce the King James Version. Yet when Eliot, alone, undertook to translate the entire Bible into the Indian language, which had never been expressed in written symbols, he could not as yet speak it. Just twenty-five years later a leather-bound copy of his translation was sent to King Charles II.

When the translation was ready for printing there was just one hand press in all British North America: that of Samuel Green in Cambridge. By August, 1635, Genesis was printed. Three years later they had to stop because the type was worn out. Eliot petitioned the General Court for help in 1660; five years later, an experienced printer with a press and new type was sent out from London, and in 1663 the work was finished.

At the coming of Eliot and his Indians, most of the land of Natick was the property of John Speen or his kindred. At Eliot's request they gave up their interest, "receiving a gratuity unto their good contentment." Thomas Sawin was the first white settler. He came from Watertown about 1685 on the request of the Indians and built a mill for grinding their corn; the white settlers were allowed to use it, but the Indians had the preference. Until 1856, and perhaps later, this property was still in the hands of descendants of the original settlers here.

Within the enclosure of the Natick Historical Society, nearly opposite the church, is the site of the Indian burial place. Here also is a monument to Eliot. The old town burying ground back of the church dates from 1731.

Professor Calvin Stowe was born in a house near by on Pleasant Street, opposite the library, and spent most of his boyhood days in Natick. He was a person of considerable achievement and distinction, but was somewhat overshadowed by his better known wife, Harriet Beecher Stowe. Her "Oldtown Folks" is a sort of composite of South Natick and the adjoining villages of Sherborn and Hopkinton. A slate tablet at the driveway to the Stowe house marks the grave of Takawambpait.

V

WAYLAND, FRAMINGHAM, AND MENDON

In 1797 there was first published at Greenfield, Massachusetts, a book of Asher Benjamin's, mostly made up of rather crude engravings of the five orders of architecture, with which were included designs for various buildings. Few, if any, of Benjamin's designs were original, however, most of them apparently having been copied from those of other architects or designers. Among other illustrations, it contained a "Design for a Church." Evidently the book had a fairly wide circulation, for with slight variations this would seem to have furnished inspiration for churches in half a dozen towns in different parts of New England. One of these is in Wayland. Its interior suffered from unfortunate alterations when the second floor was put in and the high pulpit on six columns destroyed; but the exterior, and particularly the tower and belfry, stand today as among the three or four best of their type in New England—surpassed, perhaps, only by the church in Bennington, Vermont.

At Wayland, the height of the combined tower, belfry, and cupola in relation to one another and to the whole façade, their nicety of scale and proportion, are nearly perfect, and the whole tower seems to soar aloft, pointing skywards above the level land and marshes along the river, a landmark for miles around.

Of this church, built in 1815, Andrews Palmer of Newburyport was the architect. The bell was cast in Paul Revere's foundry.

Up to 1780 Wayland was a part of the older town and parish of Sudbury. The first three meetinghouses were on the Old Burying Ground, now part of Wayland and not far away on the old Sudbury road. Sudbury was settled as early as 1638, and so this must contain the graves of some of the earliest settlers in New England. Some of these came in the *Arbella* to Sir Richard Saltonstall's settlement at Watertown, and others directly from England.

On the old moss-grown gray headstones with their queerly spelt and rudely cut inscriptions are dates covering more than two hundred and fifty years of Sudbury's and Wayland's past. The earliest is 1676. Here stood the first little meetinghouse, said, perhaps doubtfully, to have had a thatched roof. John Rutter built it, for six pounds—"three pounds to be paid in corn at three shillings a bushel, or in money . . . and the other three pounds to be paid in money, corn and cattle." The town agreed to draw all the timber to the place and to help raise the frame, though Rutter had to fell, saw, hew, and frame it, "thirty foot long, twenty foot wide"—with two "cross dorments" and six "clear story windows." Here the people were called to meeting by the town drummer, it having been agreed with Edmund Goodenow "that his son shall beat the Drum twice every lecture day, and twice every forenoon, and twice every afternoon upon the Lord's day."

It was John Rutter who, in 1651, "promised to mend the stocks"; in Sudbury as elsewhere set up near the meetinghouse. They were in use at least as late as 1722, when it was voted to "bye to pad Locks for y pound and stocks."

The first minister of this little church was Edmund Brown, of whom Captain Edward Johnson wrote, in his "Wonder-Working Providence":

> Both night and day Brown ceaseth not to watch
> Christ's little flock in pastures fresh them feed,
> The worrying wolves shall not the weak lambs catch;
> Well dost thou mind in wilderness their breed.
> Edmund, thy age is not so great but thou
> Maist yet behold the Beast brought to her fall,
> Earth's tottering Kingdome show her legs gin bow,
> Thou 'mongst Christ's Saints with prayers maist her mawle.

Wayland as a part of Sudbury was one of our oldest settlements. Besides the several garrison houses built for defense against the Indians, the meetinghouse was fortified by a stockade of logs, The town was the scene of one of the fiercest attacks of King Philip's War. On February 26, 1677, after Philip's death and when hostilities were ended, it was ordered "that such persons as have brought in logs for fortification of the meeting house, do bring in their account . . . unto the town clerk between this and the next town meeting, . . . and such as do not, shall loose both their logs, and their work, for the town will wait upon them no longer."

Two other meetinghouses followed the first little church on the site on the Old Burying Ground. In 1722 the inhabitants of the "west parish" built a new meetinghouse on Rocky Plain at Sudbury Center. About the same time the old (third) church in the burying ground was taken apart and moved to the common in the East Parish, now Wayland. There it was used until 1815, when the present "new" church was built.

It would seem that the inhabitants of Wayland did not always "walk together as becomes saints." During Jacob Bigelow's pastorate, in 1773, the town chose a committee to see what was to be done about "that set of men in this town who make it their business to trade with and cheat strangers." In compliance with which, the committee reported that "the names and characters of the persons . . . hereafter named . . . who go about the country and cheat honest men by purchasing their horses, cattle and other effects, by telling fair stories, and promising short pay, should be published in the several newspapers."

Old customs and ways of living changed but little up to the beginning of the nineteenth century. The family still sat about the great open fireplace on winter evenings and listened to tales of the Indian wars or the adventures of some returned Revolutionary soldier. Travel was mostly on horseback or on foot, and the horse block still stood before the meetinghouse. The hired man and the housemaid often were children of some of the families in town. People wore clothes made from coarse cloth their hands had spun and woven. The wooden plow was still in use, and farming and other tools were made by the village blacksmith. Eighty years ago, an old lady whose memory went back to the last years of the eighteenth century, wrote of her recollection of the old meetinghouse in the West Parish. "There was Body seats below for the oldest people And seats in the gallery for other people. The most popular took the front seats and had Pegs put up to hang their Cockt Hats on. [They] made quite a show." The deacons read two lines or a verse of the hymn as was the custom of the time, a pitch pipe being used to pitch the tune. Later, when

UNITARIAN CHURCH (1815) *Wayland, Massachusetts*

a bass viol was introduced, many of the older people greatly objected. One old gentleman took his hat from its peg and went out, saying that, now they had begun fiddling, there would be dancing next.

It was about 1828, during the pastorate of Joel Foster, that the Unitarian dissension in Wayland reached its height, and the secessionists built the Congregational church. Perhaps Mr. Foster did not take life too seriously. When his parishioners quarreled—so it is said—he played his violin. Some of the people had refused to go to church when he preached. On a Sunday morning he would saddle his horse and ride conspicuously down the main street and out of town as though on his way to exchange with a neighboring pastor. Leaving his horse tied somewhere on the outskirts, he would slip back across the fields and appear in his pulpit.

In the later years of the last century most people in Wayland were related, and the older people were called "Uncle" or "Aunt." Uncle Billy Grout, an old bachelor, lived with his sister, Aunt Susan. Uncle Billy was a Unitarian and played the organ, though Aunt Susan "went to the other church." Edmund Sears, the author of the hymn, "It came upon the midnight clear," was the minister at Wayland then, and Billy Grout perhaps was the first of the thousands of organists who have played the music to which it has been sung. The hymn was written in Wayland.

Uncle Richard Heard, dark-skinned and in later life with thick white hair, was one of the "Black Heards," said to have Indian ancestors. Old-timers in Wayland told of seeing him driving a load of hay in his shirt sleeves with high stock and dicky and a tall silk hat. His wife was known to most of the people in the village as "Aunt Richard."

The last man in Wayland to wear the farmer's blue frock, buttoned up to the neck and reaching to the knees, was Uncle Joe Ballard, who lived into the nineties of the last century. His face was always smooth-shaven, but his curling white hair fell to his shoulders. He drove a yoke of oxen. Ballard was town sexton for over forty years, and one of his duties was to toll the bell the morning after a death—three times three for a man and three times two for a woman, and then once for every year of the age of the dead.

For many years it was customary to provide gloves for the mourners. About 1773 we find:

"To James Brown, for 6 pairs of gloves for Isaac Allen's child's funeral—11 s.

"To Col. Noyes for 7 pairs gloves for Isaac Allen's burial—13 s."

The dead were buried in coffins made by the village carpenter, usually of plain pine boards colored the dull red still to be found on many old pine chests and other furniture. In 1781 a coffin made by Isaac Hunt for James Thompson "for his Father" cost ten shillings. Very different from the professional "mortician" and the "burial cases" of our day.

One of the town's ancient inhabitants of whom Alfred Wayland Cutting wrote in his delightful little book about Wayland, was "Old Man Garfield":

"At the end of the causeway across the meadows, so near the water that he could tie his boat to his woodshed . . . was the red house among the willows. . . . His life, like that of his neighbors, the minks and muskrats, whose habitations surrounded his own, was spent on the river, where his weather-beaten figure, sitting motionless and silent in his flat-bottomed boat among the lily pads, was as familiar a feature on the river as the sedge and blue-joint which lined its banks. He aspired to no higher game than horned pouts, which he neatly dressed, and, with their clean, pink bodies in a tin pail, would peddle them along the road to the village, when he went hither to get the one necessity of his life—tobacco. Selling the fish always seemed a very incidental part of these visits to town, the price being of slight account as against the favor conferred by him on the purchaser. And weren't the pouts good fried in Indian meal!

"If proper diplomacy were used in the asking, without which he probably would 'not have time,' he would put neat rush bottoms in chairs, made out of the tall green flags which bordered the river. He was the last one in the neighborhood to possess this now lost art of our grandparents. I remember the last one he did for us—how it held the green of the rushes for years."

One of Wayland's few literary lights was Lydia Maria Child, author of many once popular tales, but above all untiring in her efforts for abolition and for the United States Sanitary Commission. She and her husband lived in a little brown cottage which still overlooks the meadows through which the river winds, facing westward towards the Sudbury hills.

When the news of Gettysburg came, Mr. Child borrowed a flag from one of his neighbors, climbed a tall ash tree, lashed the staff to the topmost branch sixty feet above the ground, and with his white hair streaming in the wind sang the "Star Spangled Banner"—something of a feat for a man who must have been not far from sixty.

Each spring the Sudbury and Wayland marshes are flooded by the river, forming a lake in places two miles or more across. Before the road in the village was raised, the water would cover it, when, it is said, people coming in boats from the "Island" in the vicinity of Heard's Pond could land almost at the church steps.

During the first years of the present church, much of the traffic of the old Post Road must have passed its doors—stages from Worcester, Albany, and New York, teamsters with their covered wagons on their way from up country with produce for the Boston market, ox wagons with their yokes of slow-moving steers. Until the building of the straight road over the marshes to South Sudbury in 1815, the Post Road went from Wayland through Sudbury Center. On the opening of the Boston and Worcester turnpike through Framingham about 1810 many of the coaches took the shorter route, and finally with the coming of the railroad, a dozen years later, travel through Wayland dwindled to a single stage. But as late as the 1850's the old dusty yellow coach on alternate days was the only means of communication with Boston and the outer world. As it came into town the white-bearded old driver would whip his four horses into a gallop up the little rise to the porch in front of the old tavern. The stage steps would be let down while the cross-eyed "Buster" Allen and the other hostlers brought buckets of water from the pump under the great elm to water the horses. Meanwhile the mailbag was taken from under the driver's seat and carried across to the post office in the store; the postmaster, Mr. Seaward, and his daughters would pick out the letters for Wayland, and the coach would continue on its leisurely way to Worcester. It ran until 1881—its last trip was on the day the new railroad through South Sudbury was opened. The busy days of the old road were long passed, to be revived once more with the coming of the automobile.

At the foot of old Framingham common stands a charming little red brick church, its belfry and spire rising above a columned portico, framed between two tall maples and facing the old town hall. Within, there are white pews with doors, on either side of a center aisle and beneath the galleries, and a high pulpit with hanging sounding board much in the manner of King's Chapel or the Old North in Boston. It is a building with all the characteristics of the best work of the time of the Early Republic, but though it might well be taken for one of our older churches, it has stood for barely a quarter of a century. It was designed by the late Charles Baker, who designed or restored other buildings around the common, including many of its early houses. Originally it had been intended to add a parish house to the church, which accounts for the partially blank wall on the east side.

Though this church is the third in succession to be built on this spot, the first meetinghouse in Framingham was on a site nearly a mile away.

In 1660 and 1662 a grant of land covering most of the area of the present town of Farmingham was made to Thomas Danforth, who had come from Framlingham, Suffolk, in England. The first house within the present limits of the town was built about 1647, near the "oxbow" on the Sudbury River. By the last decade of the seventeenth century there were about seventy houses, and in 1698 the first little meetinghouse was built. At this time the place was known as Danforth's Farms.

On a little rise of ground near the river, on the old road from Framingham Centre to Framingham, once the South Village, is the Old Burying Ground, still known as the "Church Hill Cemetery." Though almost in sight of the Turnpike with its never ending stream of traffic, it is a peaceful and retired spot; and here, beneath its sheltering elms lie the early pioneers and settlers of the town—Buckminsters and Maynards, Nixons and Edgells. It was here, on the highest point of the ground, that the first meetinghouse was built: a small, unpainted building without tower or steeple, for three years unplastered inside. Men and women sat apart on either side of a central aisle, and in corresponding

FIRST PARISH CHURCH (1926) *Framingham Centre, Massachusetts*

galleries above. Under the galleries individuals were allowed to build their own pews and to cut doors to suit their own convenience. In "dignity," the "table" (deacons' seat) and the "fore seats" were accounted the highest. The front gallery equaled the second and third seats in the body of the church, those at the sides corresponding to the fourth and fifth rows on the floor. Thomas Walker and Peter Clayes were dissatisfied with their seats, but "the town" thought they "have their right[s] according to what they payed to the seventy pounds granted to repair the meeting-house." "Three weeks longer time and no more" was allowed John How "to build up his pew."

As to the younger members of the congregation, the town voted "that if the tythingmen see any youths of said town disorderly in the public worship, and they will not forbear by being once stamped at by any of the tythingmen, in such case said tythingmen are desired to call them by name."

Standing by itself in the low land near the wall at the back of the old Church Hill Cemetery, is an inconspicuous modern headstone which marks the grave of the negro slave, Peter Salem.

When, towards noon on that hot June day at Bunker Hill, Prescott's men behind the redoubt had spent their last powder, Peter Salem with others of Captain Drury's regiment was sent to their relief. Salem, it is said, had a single charge in his gun, perhaps another in his powder horn. Just then, in the language of Needham Maynard of Framingham, "I saw a British officer . . . come up with some pomp, and he cried out, 'Surrender, you damn rebels!' But Prescott . . . made a little motion with his hand, and that was the last word the Briton spoke; he fell at once." It is generally agreed that it was Peter Salem who fired the shot. Major Pitcairn fell into the arms of his son, who helped carry him to a boat lying somewhere at the foot of the hill, and to the house in Prince Street in Boston where he died.

Salem had been a slave of Captain Jeremiah Belknap of Framingham, who before the war had sold him to Major Lawson Buckminster. He served as a minute man in the company of Captain Edgell, later enlisting and serving throughout the war. As no slave could be mustered into the army, his enlistment by consent of his master amounted to emancipation.

Peter served faithfully during the war, most of the time in

Colonel Thomas Nixon's regiment, as the Colonel's bodyservant. After the war he married the granddaughter of old Nero Benson, who had been trumpeter in Captain Isaac Clark's troop in the Indian war of 1722; but his marriage proved an unhappy one, and he left Framingham and went to Leicester, where he built himself a cabin. Here he earned a precarious living by making and mending baskets, bottoming chairs, and similar odd jobs. People, especially children, liked him on account of his good nature, and his military training had given him an unfailing courtesy of manner. Straightening up, he would bring his hand up smartly to the level of his eye to salute anyone passing who greeted him. Children would gather round as he sat in the chimney corner, the flickering blaze lighting up his face while he told stories of the war and what he had seen when he "was out with Massa Nixon."

But though Peter had gone through seven years' hard service unharmed, age crept upon him at last. His erect form began to stoop; his military step grew unsteady; his thinning hair grew white. At last he was no longer able to support himself. His "settlement," as it was called, was in Framingham, and the overseers at Leicester must send him back there as the law required. He went the rounds and made a farewell visit to each of his old friends, and disappeared. His cabin fell into decay, though for many years its rough stone chimney and the lilac bushes he had planted by the door, marked its site.

On his return to Framingham, his old masters, Major Buckminster and Captain Belknap, undertook to supply his simple needs as long as he lived. Who shall say that Peter Salem, risking his life for that freedom for others which he never shared until he had won it by personal valor, does not deserve an honored place among those who have served their country well?

Not far from the road, on the southerly side of the burying ground, is the old slate headstone of Abraham Rice—"Killed by thunder sent from Heaven In seventeen hundred and seventy-seven," according to the inscription quoted from a remarkable "elegy" written by a local poetess of the time.

In 1725, the old meetinghouse in the burying ground having become rather dilapidated, steps were taken towards building a new one—an undertaking from which the most resolute might have been deterred had they foreseen the obstacles which would beset the path before the work could be brought to a conclusion.

About twenty-five years before, Joseph Buckminster, a tanner, had come to town with his family, from Muddy River (now Brookline), taking a lease of the greater part of the land granted by the General Court to Thomas Danforth. For many years Colonel Buckminster was involved in litigation over his leases of the Danforth lands, and when it was voted by a large majority to build a new meetinghouse on the site of the old one he at once registered his dissent, offering a site on land claimed as his own, though it was within the area which had been given to the town by Danforth for a church. He carried off timber which had been placed on the site and used it for the frame of his new barn. As usual, the General Court was invoked to settle the dispute. Various sites having been proposed and rejected, one was finally agreed upon, but Buckminster objected. Next he brought suit against Ephraim Bigelow, who had contracted for the frame. Another petition to the court followed, but all proved futile. Yet Colonel Buckminster served as selectman and justice of the peace, was captain in Sir Charles Hobby's regiment of grenadiers on the Port Royal expedition, and was made a colonel of militia. He was described, evidently not without reason, as a man "of resolute spirit." His son Joseph served in the French and Indian War with the rank of colonel, and a grandson was to be a major in the Revolution.

At last, after ten years of these lamentable bickerings by people who had promised by their covenant "to walk together as becomes saints," in obedience to a "presentment of the Superior Court for not having a decent meeting house," it was finally agreed to build "at an oak tree marked, standing . . . at the north end of Bare Hill." This tree stood at the northeasterly end of the common, not far from the present Congregational Church.

The site of the second meetinghouse at last having been settled, a committee to "provide" for the raising was again appointed, instructed to procure the necessary "materials" for the occasion—"one barrel of Rum, three barrels of Cyder, six barrels of Beer, with suitable provision of Meat, bread, etc." Fairly liberal, it would seem, even judged by customary standards for these events, though the conclusion of so long drawn-out a contest perhaps demanded a little extra liberality. It may be noted, however, that decision as to the quantity of materials other than liquids was left to the committee, and the voters had thoughtfully added the proviso that, "if a sufficiency of victual be brought in by particular persons, then that the town in general be not charged for the same."

The sum of £550 had been granted to build the "house" and finish the outside, with £350 additional from time to time for completing the exterior. For nearly forty years the outside was unpainted. The building faced south, across the common, with doors at the front and on each side. The pulpit was on the west, with two-story galleries on the three other sides. There were "long" seats in the main body of the church, divided by a center "alley"—the men and women being seated on either side. Two "pair of stairs" led to the galleries, where men and women were also separated. The space under the galleries was reserved for pews, to "be given to the highest payers, the several persons to enjoy their pews, provided they build the same, and finish the meeting-house against their several pews as high as the lower range of girths, within six months; the backside of the pews to be ceiled by being double-boarded up to the lower part of the windows; and then up to the girths to be boarded, lathed and plastered, and whitewashed; and at all times, keep the glass against the pews in good repair; and in case of neglect, to forfeit their pews to the town." Later permission was given "to make windows to their pews, under the inspection of the committee; the owners of said pews to provide the glass." Pews were also built by their owners in the space next to the wall in the lower front gallery. There were "long" seats in front of these. Seats in the upper gallery, finished later, were free.

The same practice was adopted to "dignify" the seats as in the first meetinghouse, except that "age was more honored—one penny being added to the assessed 'rate' of persons between fifty and sixty, . . . five pence to persons between sixty and seventy; while those over seventy were honored at the discretion of the committee." Some of the young men had already established the practice of buying "a right" with a back seat in the lower gallery, which included the privilege of placing a chair before them for their wives. The price of this privilege was three dollars and fifty cents, and in course of time it broke down the "bar" between the men's and women's seats which had existed for nearly a century.

At the time of the building of the first meetinghouse, John Swift, a young man of twenty-two or three, had come from the foot of the Blue Hills in Milton to preside over this seemingly rather unruly congregation. At first he received a salary of sixty pounds a year and his supply of firewood. The town gave him one hundred acres of farming or woodland and ten acres of meadow, to which afterwards was added a hundred pounds towards building a house. Only one-fifth of this was in "money," the rest presumably being what was commonly known as "merchantable goods." At times his salary fell into arrears, and on the squaring of accounts he would give a receipt for the amount in full "from the beginning of the world to the first of March." Once, at least, he was obliged to enter a complaint in court for nonpayment.

Mr. Swift served his people for forty-five years. Grave, yet affable and courteous, "when he received injuries at any time, he bore them with singular discretion and meekness; and the various trials and sorrows with which he was exercised . . . gave occasion for showing forth his wisdom, humility, patience and resignation to Divine will." (His wife was afflicted with periods of insanity.)

Like other well-to-do people of the town, Mr. Swift owned slaves—at one time or another, three men and two women. One of the men, Nero, the trumpeter in Captain Clark's troop in 1725, married a girl with the euphonious name of Dido Dingo. Peter Salem's wife Katy was Nero's granddaughter. A faithful servant belonging to Colonel Buckminster was Prince, who during his master's absence at the General Court had the entire management of the large farm. When towards the end of Prince's life, Buckminster offered him his freedom, he declined, saying, "Massa eat the meat; he now pick the bone." Prince lived to the age of a hundred in the family of Buckminster's son, Deacon Thomas. In his last sickness, he said he was "not afraid to be dead, but only to die."

Crispus Attucks, killed in the Boston Massacre, had been a slave in the family of Deacon William Brown. He was born in a small house which stood a little east of the military camp ground on the Turnpike, and sixty years ago the cellar hole was still to be seen. Attucks was a big mulatto, more than six feet tall. He probably was a descendant of John Attucks, an Indian taken prisoner with "Captain Tom," who lived on the hill near by, still known as Captain Tom's Hill.

In 1768, during the pastorate of Matthew Bridge, the first attempt was made to form a choir. It had been the custom for the minister to read the entire psalm, when the senior deacon would rise and, facing the congregation, repeat the first line, which would be sung; and so on to the end of the six or eight stanzas. Soon afterwards stringed instruments were introduced to "set the tune" and lead the voices. As at Sudbury, this innovation gave great offense to some of the older people, and on one occasion when the violin was disabled, one old man in an audible voice gave thanks "that the Lord's fiddle was broken." Some years later, when "Billings Collection" was first introduced and the choir sang "David the King," an aged man cried, "Hold, hold!" and, seizing his hat, rushed out of the meetinghouse. The custom of lining the psalm continued for a long time after the organizing of the choir, who found it very annoying. When Dr. David Kellogg was pastor it was the prerogative of old Deacon Brown, as senior deacon, to do this. Slowly getting up in his seat, he would adjust his glasses, clear his throat, and at last begin to read out the words. Colonel David Brewer was chorister at the time, and he struck in so quickly after Dr. Kellogg had finished reading that the deacon had no chance. After that there was no more attempt to deacon the hymn.

At one time the annual proceeds of the alewife fishery in Cochituate Brook were given to the singers. It was the custom for the voters to choose annually a committee "to regulate the singers," until 1805, when it was voted "that the singers shall regulate themselves, so long as they shall continue to . . . behave with decency and order."

It was not until 1823 that stoves were set up in the meetinghouse. Before that the women brought little tin footstoves filled with coals, and the men kept warm as best they could.

At the ordination of Dr. Kellogg in 1781, it was voted that "no extraordinary provision for a promiscuous multitude" be made, "as has been customary on such occasions; thinking the practice repugnant to the rules of the Gospel, and tends to such vain sporting as is utterly inconsistent with the solemnities of the day."

Dr. Kellogg kept up the old custom of crying the banns. The clerk would rise in his place at the afternoon service, and read: "Marriage intended—between John Smith of Boston and Keturah Jones of this town." Generally the lady found it convenient to be absent from the afternoon meeting that day.

Parson Kellogg led his people for fifty years. He lived to be eighty-seven. From his college days until he gave up active work he rose at daybreak. Always punctual, he never was five minutes late for an appointment. Rather tall, with a placid and benevolent face, he is shown in an old silhouette standing erect, walking stick in hand, dressed in the full-skirted long coat of the time, his hair in a short queue. The fine old parsonage still stands on Kellogg Street, a little beyond the river.

In 1808, during Dr. Kellogg's pastorate, the third meetinghouse was built—the first on the site of the present church. An old drawing, possibly the architect's, in the rooms of the Framingham Historical Society shows it to have been a rather plain building with two-storied, columned porch and pediment, and tower and belfry of three stages with a short spire and weathervane. It stood until 1847, to be followed by the wooden pseudo-Gothic church which was burnt on the evening of Easter Monday, 1920. This in turn was replaced by the present brick building—the fifth of the First Parish (Unitarian), and the third on this site—one of the most beautiful small churches in the style of the Federal period and the only modern church which we shall describe.

It was in Dr. Kellogg's later years that the Unitarian movement in New England reached its height and the orthodox members of the parish broke away and built the Congregational church dedicated in 1830, which, remodeled and altered, stands today on the opposite side of the common. The wooden shell of this building now covers the structure of the original meetinghouse.

Today the white meetinghouse built by the Baptists, which faces the little maple-shaded green between Pleasant Street and

BAPTIST CHURCH (1825) *Framingham Centre, Massachusetts*

the Turnpike, is the only survival of the town's church architecture of the period of the Early Republic.

In 1612, in the reign of King James I of England and VI of Scotland—that droll character and eccentric monarch whose name is inseparably connected with the best loved version of the English Bible—there came to England from Holland the chief follower of the Reverend John Smyth. Smyth was a Church of England clergyman who had founded a church "of English people remaining in Amsterdam in Holland . . . to receive all their members by baptism upon the confession of their faith and sins," with the doctrine "that baptism in no way appertaineth to infants." Smyth died in Holland, but his chief follower established a little church in London. This was the origin of the Baptist denomination in England.

By 1772 there were enough disciples of Smyth in Framingham to hold meetings in the upper part of Ebenezer Marshall's tavern at Park's Corner. Soon they bought a meetinghouse that had been built by certain dissenting members of the First Parish, but had later been abandoned.

David Fiske, one of the leading members of the Baptist church, left his whole estate to it, and in 1825, with this as a nucleus, sufficient funds were raised to build a new meetinghouse. Solomon Willard of Boston was the architect, and Colonel Daniel Harrington of Shrewsbury the builder. On the first Sunday of January, 1827, the present building was dedicated.

Though the balustrades above the tower and belfry stages were damaged in the 1938 hurricane and have not been replaced, the spire is still quite satisfactory, and with the fine Ionic portico and pediment the exterior stands as a charming example of the New England meetinghouse of the period. Unfortunately, in various repairings and refurnishings, the pulpit and other original fittings were removed, and the congregation now faces a blank wall, looking in vain for the high pulpit with crimson cushion and flanking stairways with delicately molded rail and balusters which lent grace to many early buildings. The church originally had a separate gallery with seats for the negroes, reached by separate stairs.

Until 1811 various preachers rather irregularly "supplied the desk"—among them one Elisha Rich, a gunsmith by trade. In that year the church was incorporated and there came to it Charles Train, first of a family of considerable note, that was to serve the town and state in various capacities.

Train had been in Framingham since 1807 as "Preceptor" of the Framingham Academy—the old stone building on the common, now occupied by the Framingham Historical Society. As his services were "eminently acceptable, and the Academy prospered under his direction," the trustees apparently felt that the one shilling a week which his scholars paid for tuition was not overliberal, for they contributed fifty cents weekly towards his board. During the cold weather the pupils were charged six cents a week for fuel.

During his pastorate of nearly thirty years Mr. Train served the town for several sessions in the General Court and the State Senate, though it is recorded that he was "allowed to stay at home" during one session, for having, as he believed, preached two sermons on temperance "of a more stringent character than at the time suited the taste of the people." Evidently he was ahead of his time, for in those days most clergymen and their congregations liked their toddy. In many houses a little of the best Jamaica was set aside for the day when the parson might come to call, and a wise young pastor learned to know about how many calls he could make in an afternoon.

Twenty-seven years after Charles Train gave up his pastorate, his son, Arthur Savage Train, received a call to his father's old church.

Family records give an amusing account of Arthur's younger brother Charles R. When Charles was eight years old, his father took both boys to see the laying of the corner stone of Bunker Hill Monument:

"With the old mare harnessed into the yellow-hulled chaise, my father, brother and myself travelled to Boston, making the distance of twenty-one miles in four hours. I was gorgeously arrayed in a green bombazine frock and trousers and ruffled collar. My hat was made of Dunstable braid, nicely plaited by the fingers of my loving mother, and made into a hat by one of our neighbors. . . . My feet were dressed in bootees from leather tanned and manufactured in Framingham, and shining with black-ball, well laid on for the journey. . . . Arrived in Boston, I thought my hat not quite the thing for such an occasion, and my indulgent parent bought me my first cap of John M. Peck, who kept a famous hat-store at the corner of Cornhill and Washington streets, and my straw hat was consigned to the chaise-box.

"The following morning we went to Roxbury, and near the old Punch-bowl Tavern we first saw Lafayette, my father holding me up in his arms that I might see the procession over the heads of the crowd,—my brother, five years older, being able to take care of himself.

"I can see Lafayette in my mind's eye as distinctly as I saw him then; and were I gifted with the pencil I could paint a perfect likeness of him as he appeared in the barouche in which he rode, receiving the honors and congratulations accorded to him by a grateful and enthusiastic people. I wore upon that occasion on my breast a badge of white satin ribbon, on which was printed the likeness of Lafayette, and beneath it the motto, 'Welcome Lafayette!'

"At the laying of the corner-stone of the Monument, I was so near Mr. Webster as to see him distinctly and to hear his voice; and the scene with Mr. Webster upon the platform and Lafayette sitting among the veterans is burned into my memory."

Of the hats of home manufacture which he thought "not quite the thing" he says: "Many an hour have I spent in the chimney-corner braiding straw, for which I received three-quarters of a cent a yard,—my stint being two yards in the morning and two in the afternoon." The manufacture of straw hats later became an important industry in Framingham.

A son of Charles R. Train—Charles J.—became an admiral in the navy, but it was reserved for the youngest, who, like his father and grandfather had been bred to the law, to achieve a world-wide fame of a kind unthought of by any of these serious-minded forebears of the Church and Law. Perhaps it was just as well, for in all probability they would have strongly disapproved of him. "The alleged parents of Ephraim [Tutt] are, in fact, my paternal uncle, the Rev. Arthur Savage Train, a Baptist clergyman, and his wife," said his creator. Though born in Boston instead of Framingham, Arthur Train seized upon the old "Centre Square" of his ancestral town—now, alas, changed beyond recognition—as the center of the famous Pottsville: "He had vaguely recalled the town as a cluster of low wooden and red-brick buildings—a blacksmith shop, a tavern, a few high-stooped stores [he had spent his life in New York] and a bank, at the turn of a narrow, dusty road beside an embowered 'common,' the tops of whose fanlike elms were pierced by several spires. To his memory it had been as sleepy as 'Sleepy Hollow' itself. Now, in place of the winding uneven country road, there lay a smooth ribbon of level concrete over which motors were humming in continuous streams in both directions."

"More especially he was looking for his grandfather's meeting-house,—the white wooden, Wrenn [sic] meeting-house with narrow green blinds and tall thin spire, set in the grove of maples, where his grandfather had preached more than a century ago."

"The caw of a crow in the near-by branches belittled the honk of the motors beyond the turn. On the farther side of the knoll the ancient horse-sheds still offered an unaccepted and unnecessary hospitality. . . . The inside was almost chill in contrast to the warmth of the afternoon outside, faintly sweet with the odor of dried timber, empty, save for the shadowy presences who seemed to throng the aisles and fill the pews about him. His eyes ran over the long rows to the pulpit where his grandfather had preached from 1811 to 1839, and the uncle, for whom he had been named, from 1866 to 1872.

"For over a century its clanging bell had summoned its congregation to Sunday worship or tolled for the passing of the village fathers,—from the days of John Quincy Adams to those of Herbert Hoover. What incredible changes it had witnessed; from the stage coach to the motor car, the aeroplane and the submarine; . . . from the handloom to the automatic repairing machine for silk stockings!"

In one of Judge Sewall's interleaved "almanacks" may be found these truly Pepysian entries:

"Dec. 29 1675. Mr. Rayner came in the evening to our house [and] delivered me a letter. Lodged here; in bed we had much and varied discourse."

"Dec. 30. Mr. R. goes on his journey."

This was John Rayner, the first minister of Mendon.

In 1668 it had been voted that "the Meeting house shall be

sett on the highest side or pte of the land wch is a High way neere Joseph White's saw pit, in his howse lott, and to erect it with all speede." And here it was built by Job Hide, for "the best And cheapest Tearmes" the Selectmen could get, "the breadth 22 foote square, 12 foote studd, the Ruffes gathered to A 7 foote square wth a Turrett."

The "best And cheapest Tearmes" were 2s. 6d. per day.

This, the first of four meetinghouses which preceded the one we see today, was burnt when the town was attacked and fired by the Indians in King Philip's War.

In 1680 Grindall Rawson was called to the parish. Rawson's father Edward Rawson, had first settled in Newbury, where he held various offices, later being elected Secretary to the Colony. On coming to Boston he lived in Rawson's Lane, now Bromfield Street. Born in Gillingham, Dorsetshire, in 1615, he married Rachel Perne, a granddaughter of John Hooker, whose wife was a sister of Edmund Grindal, Archbishop of Canterbury in the reign of Elizabeth.

One is tempted to transcribe some of the records of the building of the earlier meetinghouses, if only for their extraordinary spelling of an age when town clerks were untrammeled by any of the later rules imposed by Webster or Worcester. For the second building, built during Rawson's pastorate, Samuel Hayward did "ingage to begine and manige the frame . . . calling in what helpe hee sese convenient." Hayward was to be allowed 3 shillings a day, and the selectmen were "to procure him a Cow with a calf or a calf by her side, as soon as the frame is raised," as part of his pay. Abraham Staples engaging "to pay the cow if no other be procured. . . . If help fail him . . . to have pay produced to procure help, . . . and to take the Cow at the price that 2 indifferent men shall prize her." Under which amicable arrangement, including we trust, the paying of the cow, the meetinghouse was built, though not without the usual preliminary disagreement as to the choice of a site.

The third meetinghouse came in 1690, while Grindall Rawson still was pastor. Though it was used for nearly fifty years, the site, strangely, is unknown.

In 1684, "att a general towne metting of the Inhabitants," Mr. Rawson's salary had been raised from twenty pounds a year with "bord and hors" to "Fifty five pounds to bee paid as followeth, fifteen pounds per annum in Starling money of New England and forty pounds more to be paid in good marchantabell country pay such as the town Rayseth." Besides which they were to give him a forty-acre "lott, one Cord of wood yerely . . . to be delivered att his dore." His "Sallery" is to be paid "upon the twenty fift October and the twenty fift of March," the "good marchantabell country pay" consisting of pork, wheat, barley, and other goods, including two pounds of butter from every cow—a form of payment in kind that would be quite acceptable now, something over two centuries and a half later.

For several years during Rawson's ministry Deacon Warfield was allotted fifteen shillings for sweeping the meetinghouse—"thirty feet square & no pews"—to be assessed with the minister's salary.

During this period we find entries in the town records of a long drawn-out controversy with James Bick, a blacksmith.

Bick had agreed to do the town's "smithery work"; and when he neglected to comply with his agreement or to pay fifteen pounds for his shortcoming, the constable was directed "to warn James Bick forthwith" to take off the frame he had erected for his house and his fence from the town's land, "and no more to In Comber the same."

In 1728 the town again voted to build a new meetinghouse—the fourth—when for eight years a long drawn-out controversy as to site and other contingent matters prevailed, the building not being finished until 1736. At one time feeling between the factions ran so high that someone "damnified the Meeting House" by attempting to cut off one of the corner posts—an act that was verified when the building was taken down in 1846. As early as 1730, however, a committee was chosen "to take care of the Victuals and Drink & other materials necessary for Raising the New Meeting House." The "other materials" would seem to have been of secondary importance; but, lest there be any doubt as to the second item, it was definitely voted that it be a barrel of "Rhum."

To extract anything beyond dry facts from most of our New England town histories or "annals" requires more than a little imagination; yet, if we could but read between the lines, among the records of votes at countless town meetings there must lie hidden many a tale of human interest and romance. Who was the James Bick who for nearly ten years was such a thorn in the flesh of the town fathers, and why, having brought letters of recommendation acceptable to them and been given a ten-acre lot "with all the privileges belonging to the same," did he suddenly refuse to do the town's smithery work? What were the charms of Ruth Bundy, recorded as the widow of John Gurney, on the town's books for unpaid taxes in 1683, and whom Matthias Puffer "took from Mendon when the town gave him liberty" during the Indian troubles "to go to Braintree to look after his children"? As it appears that Ruth was thrice married it would seem that her charms were more than ordinary. Gurney is thought to have been killed by the Indians in the massacre and burning of Mendon in 1675. During these raids on the town, poor John More, one of Mr. Rawson's parishioners, was impressed with his horse to go to Marlborough with supplies for the "soulders" under Captain Henchman, and "in ye night coming home, being very dark," was much bruised and fell into the river.

As the records show More to have been ninety-five years old or thereabouts, it is not clear why he was chosen for the important and arduous duty of carrying three hundred and twenty pounds of beef and other heavy supplies to Marlborough, some twenty miles distant. At that time the only means of communication between the settlements was by rough forest paths; that between Mendon and Marlborough was no doubt an Indian trail, a link between the Connecticut and Bay paths. This probably would have led him past the Indian lands on Magunco Hill, now part of Ashland. It was in the late fall or winter, and by the time More reached that part of the path which passed through or near the site of the present town of Milford, it would have been night, and as he said, very dark. It probably was the Mill River, which crosses the present road at Hopedale, into which he fell and was so "much bruised" that he became "very sick and weak." Within two miles of Mendon, he had ridden forty miles over a rough and poorly marked path through the woods, the first half of his journey on a heavily laden horse and the last part in the darkness of a November night.

After Mendon was deserted following the Indian attack, More

went to Medfield, where he says he was severely wounded by the Indians. His petition for "something for his cow, corn and peas delivered to Captain Henchman" and for a small pension for his relief "in that little time he hath to live in this world" would seem to have been justified.

As in other towns, the stocks and whipping post probably were set up near the meetinghouse, and all idle and disorderly persons were punished by "moderate whipping or setting in the stocks." Unfortunates in the Work House who did not perform "such reasonable task or stint as was set them" were included among the disorderly. Those were the days when the Work House *was* the work house, not yet disguised as the Town Farm; in a more sophisticated age to be replaced by the all-inclusive Social Security. That no lack of the constable's time-honored emblem of office should be lacking, we find that Town Clerk Samuel Read lent ten shillings to "prcuer black staff." By law the constable was to have his staff with him when in discharge of his duties, "so that none could plead ignorance." We are reminded of Hardy's story of "The Three Strangers":

"But I can't do nothing without my staff—can I, William, and John, and Charles Jake? No; for there's the king's royal crown a painted on en in yaller and gold, and the lion and the unicorn, so as when I raise en up and hit my prisoner, 'tis made a lawful blow thereby. I wouldn't 'tempt to take up a man without my staff—no, not I. If I hadn't the law to gie me courage, why, instead o' my taking up him he might take up me!"

The "New Meeting House," the fifth, which stands on its little green today, was built in 1820. The old building getting dilapidated "and also entirely out of fashion, having no spire, tower or bell," a meeting was called to consider the matter of building a new one. Enos, Elijah, and Amariah Taft, all members of the family of the future President, were among the twelve composing the committee to "contract with some skillfull architect for the erection and completion of said building and make themselves personally liable for the amount of the consideration to be paid said architect for the erection and completion of said building." The fund totaled $6,460, Jonathan Russell at $830 being the largest subscriber.

Elias Carter of Worcester was the "skillfull architect," a man

PORCH OF THE OLD CHURCH (1820) *Mendon, Massachusetts*

of outstanding ability for his time, probably a member of that "United Fraternity of Architects in the North District of the County of Worcester" who, in that war year of 1812, were meeting at the Templeton Inn. Elias's father had been a church builder and was killed by a fall from the meetinghouse he was building in Leicester. Elias was twenty-four when, in 1805, he built the church at Brimfield. Fifteen years later he designed and built the Mendon church. One whole side of the frame was raised at a time, Carter standing, it is said, on the top girth of the first side and going up with it.

At a meeting of the building committee it had been voted "that no person be permitted to sell spirituous liquors on the meeting house common, or in the public highway near it, on the days of raising said House, and that the committee shall prosecute any who shall violate this rule." A decided innovation in a day when it was the custom to grant special privileges for the sale of liquor at church raisings.

The church we see today is little changed from the building Carter left a century and a quarter ago. The front, with its delicately scaled columns and pediment, is well proportioned, and the details of the cornice and spire are refined. Within, the doors of all the paneled pews are still in place. Stairs from the vestibule lead to galleries at sides and rear, those at the sides with their many pews indicating that when the church was built there was a large congregation.

But the pulpit is the striking feaure of the interior. One might perhaps wish it a little taller in its proportions, as of the earlier time when high pulpits were more in vogue, and though the elaborate arch-and-fan motif is but little related to the blank wall back of it and to the flanking windows, one may well believe that it was the pride of the architect, who it is said used to stay after the workmen had gone, to study its proportions and work upon it. All together, I think we may agree that there also he deserved that praise which building committees are by no means always ready to bestow, but which was voted by the parish at near-by Milford, whose church he also built: "That the thanks of the Parish be given Mr. Elias Carter . . . for his able and faithful performance of his trust in erecting the meeting house this day accepted by the said Parish." To which the pastor added:

"The above was deservedly presented to Mr. Carter, a skillful and faithful architect and amiable and pious man." Unfortunately the Milford church has been marred by injudicious remodeling.

Mendon today is still a pleasant New England village with an old town hall, a country store and post office, and the remains of an ancient wheelwright and blacksmith shop. Many charming old white houses remain, not very much encroached upon by modern machine-made architecture. And Elias Carter's white church still stands well back from the Boston turnpike, its ancient horse sheds still there, overshadowed by an enormous elm tree unscathed by two hurricanes.

VI

SHREWSBURY, LANCASTER, AND GROTON

SHREWSBURY of course takes its name from the old English town not far from the Welsh border, famous for its black and white timbered houses and its boys' school and the battle in which Henry IV defeated the Earl of Northumberland and his Welsh and Scottish allies, and Falstaff fought Hotspur "a long hour by Shrewsbury clock." Aside from the fact that both towns are "set upon a hill," the old and the new would seem to have little in common.

Of late years the Massachusetts town has become something of a suburb of Worcester, and modern houses occasionally encroach upon the older ones along the village street; but it still retains much of its early charm as a New England village. All about are rolling hills and farm lands, and from the newer part of the burying ground near the church there is a charming view across the valley towards the Boylston hills, with Wachusett rising above them in the distance.

Among New England settlements Shrewsbury is not an old town, for it was not until 1717 that the grant was made to the first forty families "provided they . . . build themselves houses, and settle an orthodox minister within three years"; but during these nearly two and a half centuries the church has had only two buildings—unusual in New England, where neighboring towns were continually tearing down and rebuilding their more or less hastily constructed wooden meetinghouses.

By the end of the time allowed, the "Town proprietors," meeting at the house of the widow How in Marlborough, chose a committee to "manage about the setting up of the meeting-house." The setting up of two sawmills was an important part of the "managing," and in 1721 the first meetinghouse was built on Rocky Pine Plain, just a little northeast of the present church.

In 1766 it had become too small for the growing congregation, and there were demands from the people of the south part of the town to have the new meetinghouse nearer. The usual petition went to the General Court, but this was finally withdrawn and the church was built on Rocky Plain near the old one. Daniel Heminway, who had come to Shrewsbury from Framingham and was well known as a church builder, was the architect. Later he framed the Northborough church and the old South in Worcester. Timbers were cut in Shrewsbury woodlands, and Shrewsbury blacksmiths made the nails. All being ready, the town having voted to provide the "necessary"—a barrel of rum from Boston—the frame was raised, after which all hands sat down to a good supper. July 13, 1766, Joseph Sumner, the minister, wrote in his journal: "Being Lord's Day we met ye first time in the new House, upon wh. occasion I preached from Genesis 28 chapter & ye 17 verse—'this is none other but the house of God, and this is the gate of Heaven.' "

For forty-two years the building had no steeple or bell. The long side with the principal entrance porch faced the south, and there were smaller porches on each end at the east and west. The pulpit faced the broad aisle opposite the principal entrance, and galleries extended around the three other sides, the choir being in the south gallery. In 1807 the tower and steeple were built in the place of the west porch. The high square pews with hinged seats to allow more standing room when the people rose to sing, remained until 1834, when they and the fine high pulpit were taken out. At this time the building was turned around to face the south and the "vestry" built underneath. The south and east porches were removed and sold—the large south porch to be used for a while as a workshop, later to be moved again to a house on the Goulding Hill road where it stood for many years, "somewhat changed by time and the carpenter."

Saddest of all, perhaps, was the removal of the old pulpit, and the substitution of one of "handsome mahogany," designed by the Reverend Mr. Allen. Jacob Abbott wrote a long description of it in the *Religious Magazine:* "It is a beautiful pier table, placed upon a platform a little elevated above the congregation, and more perfectly corresponds with our idea of what a pulpit should be than anything else we have ever seen. There is an air of ease and elegance about it which we have never before seen in the most costly specimens of pulpit architecture." Delegates from adjoining towns were sent to look upon this remarkable work of art. But having been made in Framingham and delivered on a Saturday night, it was installed in its place on the Sabbath morning, and Mr. Allen refused to conduct the service from it because the labor had been performed on the Lord's day, and the people repaired to the hall as usual.

Not many years ago the interior of the church was once more remodeled. Fortunately the work was put into the hands of a competent architect, and although here as with so many of our old churches, it is greatly to be regretted that much of the original work had been destroyed, with the present high pulpit and reading desk the interior has an architectural character and charm all too rare in the "restoration" of old New England churches. It is most gratifying too, to note that the steeple blown off in the 1938 hurricane was promptly replaced.

As we have seen, there was no permament settlement in Shrewsbury until 1717; but a grant of land had been made nearly a hundred years earlier to a young Englishman, Isaac Johnson, who probably never saw Shrewsbury. In 1628 he and his beautiful young wife, the Lady Arbella, a daughter of the Earl of Lincoln, sailed for Boston in the little ship named in her honor. The "stately ship *Arbella*" was a small, high-sterned and clumsily rigged little vessel that tossed about on the waves of the Atlantic and must have seemed anything but that. For a time the frail young wife found a home with friends in Salem; but, used to the comforts of a great English house, she soon succumbed to the hardships of a New England winter and her broken-hearted husband survived her only a month. His grave is said to have been the first in the new King's Chapel burying ground.

Here as elsewhere in New England, the name of old Judge Sewall bobs up to confront us. His father-in-law the mintmaster had a grant of land in Shrewsbury, which, along with the pinetree shillings, he presented to his daughter on her marriage to Sewall. This came to the Judge on her death; and a hill and a pond in Shrewsbury bear his name to this day.

Though the first little meetinghouse was raised in 1721, it was two years before a settled minister was installed, in December of 1723. Born in Hingham and graduated from the college at Cambridge in 1714, Job Cushing was a grandson of Matthew Cushing, who with his wife and five children had come from Norfolk in England to Hingham in 1638, three years after Peter Hobart and his party. Job built his parsonage on his grant of land and in 1727 married a daughter of John Prentice, his neighbor, who was minister of the church in Lancaster. He had received sixty pounds "settlement," and by this time his sixty pounds a year had been increased to sixty-eight, so that he doubtless kept a horse; and we can imagine him traveling the twelve miles or more by the old road over the hills through Boylston, crossing the river somewhere in the valley now filled by the waters of the Wachusett Reservoir. The parsonage, described as a fine house for the times, was a little east of the town hall, where it stood for a hundred years, when Cushing's successor, George Allen, built another on the same site.

Cushing preached to the people of Shrewsbury for nearly forty years. Binding sheaves in his field one August day in 1760, he was overcome by the heat, and died before help could reach him.

After his death there came to Shrewsbury a young man destined for more than sixty years to hold a foremost place in the affections of the people of his church and throughout the town.

About the middle of the eighteenth century eight young men had set out on horseback from their native town of Pomfret in Connecticut, to Yale College. With them was a lad of ten, Oliver Grosvenor, the brother of one of them, who was to bring back the horses. The procession attracted considerable attention as it passed through the village, and a lady from Massachusetts who was visiting in Pomfret asked what was to be done with all these young men. "We are going to send them as missionaries into Massachusetts," was the answer—and six of them afterwards became pastors of Massachusetts churches.

One of the ten young men was Joseph Sumner. He was graduated with honors in the class of 1759, and, like many young graduates of the time, taught school for a term before preparing for the ministry. Three years later he accepted a call to Shrewsbury and was duly installed as pastor. One of his first acts in honor of the occasion was to have his hair cut short and to put on a wig—requisite to the dignity of his position according to the fashion of the time; and thereafter he never appeared in public without it. The following year he bought Artemas Ward's house near the church and married Miss Lucy Williams of Pomfret, "a worthy young lady of great refinement and intelligence, from an ancient and noted family," and "We came to live at our own house."

Sumner's pastorate covered all of the stormy period of the Revolution, and the years in which those "dark clouds of doctrinal controversy" passed over New England. His sermons are said to have been "attractive, not being so long as to be wearisome," which may in some measure account for the large congregations that necessitated the building of the larger church in 1766.

"Of a commanding figure which he carried with great dignity" (he was six feet four inches in height), with dark piercing eyes, "mentally he was strong, calm, and equal to all emergencies." For sixty-two years he held a prominent place in the affairs of the town. Forty-seven of them he lived with his beloved wife—his "amiable consort" of whom he wrote, "Her domestic virtues were equalled by few, excelled by none." For thirty-four years they occupied the Artemas Ward house. The latter part of his life was spent in the fine old house still standing west of the church, which is still occupied by his descendants.

On the streets of the town in full white wig and three-cornered hat, or looking down from the pulpit in black gown and muslin bands, Mr. Sumner must have been an awe-inspiring figure at least to the younger members of his congregation; yet, like others of his calling in that age and generation, he enjoyed a social glass or two with friends, and it was expected that he should have it. It is told that once, when he had come to make a pastoral call, the rum bottle was found to be empty and a boy was sent in haste to borrow from a neighbor. One of the great tumblers now so prized by collectors, full to the brim and not too much diluted with sweetened water, was passed first to the reverend and honored guest. Taking it in his hand, he told a story, took a few modest sips, and passed it to the other caller, Captain Thomas Knowlton. Knowlton told his story, took a drink, and passed it to the host, who followed in his turn. Three times it passed from hand to hand and from hand to mouth, each time inspiring more zest in the story-teller. It is to be regretted that there is no record of the stories, particularly of the last round.

Captain Knowlton had a dog strongly suspected of sheep killing. Like most dog owners he was of course convinced that Ranger could not be guilty of any such crime; so sure, in fact, that he was only too anxious to prove the dog's innocence. Ranger spent the night on the hearth in his master's bedroom and was always there in the morning when Knowlton awoke. The latter slept with a window open over a roof which sloped so low that the dog could reach the ground. One night Knowlton went to bed but not to sleep, and after a while Ranger crept to the window and disappeared, returning several hours later and taking his usual place by the fire. The next morning he was gone from the neighborhood, never to be seen or heard of again. Just what happened is left to our surmise.

Knowlton was something of a musician and for many years led the church choir. His house, inherited from his father, was burnt during the first years of the Revolution. Nails then were particularly hard to obtain, and they managed to get only enough to build a small house on the site. Neighbors gave them seeds to plant a garden. Many of these were tied up in bits of cloth, and these small pieces were so precious that the mother sewed them together for a dishcloth.

Dr. Sumner was without an assistant until three or four years before his death. George Allen came to the church in that capacity, and in due course he was installed as pastor, remaining for seventeen years, when he removed to Worcester. It was during the later years of Allen's pastorate that the most drastic changes were made in the church.

Shrewsbury had the prevailing trouble with churchgoing dogs, and Mr. Allen decided that for him, at least, the time had come to dispense with them—a decision prompted by the incident of old Ben Stone and the tavern-keeper Balch Dean's dog. *

Evidently Allen was a reformer, for it was he who decided that there should be less toddy at funerals. It had been the custom in New England to provide refreshment for the bearers,

---

* Related in "Coaching Roads of Old New England."

THE CHURCH (1766) FROM THE OLD BURIAL GROUND *Shrewsbury, Massachusetts*

CHURCH OF THE FIRST PARISH (1816) *Lancaster, Massachusetts*

and while the mourners sat in the parlor the toddy sticks twirled in the kitchen. At the next funeral, the minister stopped the service and suddenly appeared in the kitchen. Thereafter, there was no more toddy at funerals.

Until the town hall was built in 1872, town meetings were held in the "vestry" under the church and bakers sold buns and gingerbread to the voters. Here also were given the old Lyceum lectures, and the walls of the hall resounded to the speeches of famous orators of the day, among them the young Senator Hoar, just entering public life, who delivered an address on the Fugitive Slave Law.

But with little doubt General Artemas Ward was Shrewsbury's "favorite son." Soldier, merchant, lawyer; representative in the General Court, chief justice; but above all soldier; for many years when not away in the service of his country in war or in peace, he and his wife, a great-granddaughter of Increase Mather, occupied a pew on the broad aisle of the church on Sunday. To be sure, it was not just the same broad aisle, for, as we have seen, since that time the old building has been a good bit changed and the door in the south porch through which the General and his lady entered has entirely disappeared.

The fine old house where General Ward lived for much of his life, and where he died, stands at the foot of the hill on the Post Road, once the King's Highway, as the town is approached from Northborough. A monument in front of the house tells us of his services during the Revolution, when a third of the able-bodied men of Shrewsbury were in the war. Among other things, Ward suggested and directed the fortification of Dorchester Heights. He was the first general in the Colonial army to receive his commission by American authority.

In 1785 General Ward built the west end of the house for himself, leaving the old part for his son Thomas, afterward high sheriff of Worcester County—then an office of considerable importance. Thanks to the generosity of one of General Ward's descendants, the house is now in the possession of Harvard College and is open to the public. It is appropriately furnished with many of the family possessions, including portraits and other articles of interest.

The old town of Lancaster, one of the most charming of Massachusetts towns, is fortunate in the possession of one of the most notable churches of the period of the Early Republic.

It is situated on a hill about whose foot sweep the two uniting branches of the Nashua, and the green, orchard-clad slopes of the Bolton and Harvard hills roll up in the east beyond the intervale, with Wachusett blue in the distance on the western horizon. Though the first settlers chose the lower site near the "Meeting of the Waters" the higher land later became the Center village, and here, halfway along the elm-shaded village street, their descendants built the beautiful meetinghouse that stands today.

The church of the First Parish at Lancaster has been called Bulfinch's masterpiece, and he certainly displayed creative genius and originality in the combination of the various features of his design, for the building is unique among American churches of the period. For many years much of the beauty of line and detail of the exterior was lost in the drab-colored paint of the cupola and other wood finish, but in recent years the white paint of the woodwork has again revealed the full merit of the original design.

Certain changes have been made in the interior since the church was built, but the first thing which meets the eye is the beautiful pulpit, as fine as any of its type in America. It is thought that Jacob Fisher, a Lancaster man and a skillful cabinetmaker, may have carved the capitals of the eight Ionic columns and four pilasters. When the Thayer Memorial Chapel was built in 1881, the arched window at the back of the pulpit was closed up, the crimson draperies hung in its place and doors cut on each side. Two windows on each side of the pulpit had previously been closed, very likely on account of the unpleasantly strong light in the eyes of the congregation. A few changes were made in the gallery when the organ was put in. The seating is much as it originally was installed.

For twenty-four years the church had no organ. The present organ, of remarkably fine tone, replaces an earlier one. The bell was made by Paul Revere.

In 1869 this beautiful church narrowly escaped one of those acts of vandalism perpetrated on many New England churches about this time. It was proposed to put in a floor at the level of the galleries, making a lower "vestry" and utterly destroying the proportions of the whole interior. To the "courageous and vigorous stand" of Mr. Bartol, minister at that time, the church and all who appreciate the best in New England architecture of the period are everlastingly indebted.

Competent authorities interested in the church felt that, if the funds had been sufficient, the architect would have given some adequate treatment to the walls and ceiling in harmony with the rest of the interior, and in 1900, after careful study of similar work in other buildings by Bulfinch, the panels with ornamented moldings were installed, including the decorative plaster work on the ceiling.

It is said that there is no record of Bulfinch's ever being in Lancaster, and it seems likely that the "Captain Thomas Hersey" (not a resident of Lancaster) who is referred to in the town records as "master builder," and by the town's historian, Marvin, as "the architect," probably interpreted Bulfinch's plans and superintended the work, for which he received five hundred dollars. Hersey was an associate or assistant of Bulfinch's.

This is the fifth meetinghouse built by the people of the First Parish in Lancaster. The town, first called Nashaway, was one of those which suffered particularly severely from the Indian raids of King Philip's War. The first few settlers came from Watertown and that neighborhood about 1643, doubtless by the Bay Path. Soon they called a young university graduate named Norcross as minister; but he soon left them "for their delays" and, it is thought, returned to England.

Among the first permanent settlers was Joseph Rowlandson, who in 1654 became the first settled pastor; he was destined to play a prominent part in the community's early tragedy. His house, which was also the garrison house, was on a knoll above the low land on the west side of the road to South Lancaster, just beyond the bridge over the North Branch. The first little meetinghouse was across the road "near the eastern brow of cemetery hill." On the morning of the 10th of February, 1676, came the attack of the Indians when the village was burnt and many of the inhabitants killed. Mrs. Rowlandson and three of the children were carried off. The story of their hardships on their journey in midwinter over the snow was vividly told in her account of the twenty "removes," until they were brought back to the vicinity of Wachusett and finally rescued. After the destruction of the town, Rowlandson was settled in Wethersfield, Connecticut, where he died in 1678.

Gradually the inhabitants returned, and in 1684–85 a new meetinghouse was built on the same site, to which John Whiting came in 1690. Both he and Andrew Gardner, who arrived in 1701, met tragic deaths, evidence of the constant anxiety and fear in which the inhabitants of all these early frontier towns must have lived. Whiting was surprised by the Indians at a distance from the garrison house in the attack of September, 1697, and killed. On the 6th of November, 1704, a party of Indians was discovered at Still River and the soldiers and inhabitants of Gardner's garrison went in pursuit. They found no Indians and returned at night tired by the long march. Gardner offered to stand the watch. Samuel Prescott, "between sleeping and waking," heard him come out of the little watch house late at night and, probably taking him for an Indian, shot and mortally wounded him. In the same year the new meetinghouse was burnt.

By this time the principal settlement was on the "East Side," at the Old Common, and after much opposition and the usual lengthy discussions and petitions to the General Court, the third building was placed in 1706 on the south side of the Bolton Road opposite the Old Common burying ground, not far from the present Industrial School for Girls, where it stood until 1743.

Petitions for property damage and for wounds and illness incurred in the war were made to the General Court, though expenses for care of the sick and aged and other "relief" were borne in part by the town. This was the bill for the sickness and funeral in 1704 of John Carter, a Lancaster soldier:

To two journeys to Concord for ye Doctor	01. 7s. od.
one " " Boston for things for said Carter in his sickness,	0–11–0
Nursing one week,	0–10–0
4 Gallons rum,	0–15–7
½ a barrel Syder,	0–4–0

Sugar, fruit and spice,	0-5-6
6 pair of Gloves,	0-9-0
ye Coffin and Grave,	0-8-0

Nathaniel Sawyer, Ephriam Wilder.

The eleven shillings for "one journeys to Boston for things" seem reasonable enough, and certainly the ten shillings for nursing one week; but the four gallons of rum and half-barrel of "Syder" would seem to have been liberal, even for an eighteenth century funeral.

Two long pastorates followed Gardner's. In 1705 John Prentice began to preach; and for nearly forty years, until his death in 1748, he served his people in Lancaster—most of the time in the meetinghouse on the Old Common.

By the last years of Prentice's pastorate the town had increased in population and area to such an extent that it was voted to build two new meetinghouses. The usual petitions and discussions as to sites having been disposed of (some wanting to return to the site near the old burying ground), it was finally agreed to leave the Old Common and put the larger building on Schoolhouse Hill and the smaller on Ridge Hill. In our own time when for many years carpenters have never picked up a dropped nail, it is interesting to note that it was voted in town meeting to "pull off ye clapboard and nails of ye old meetinghouse, and divide them betwixt ye Precincts according to ye pay." Nails that had to be hammered out by hand were worth picking up—even at a price.

Throughout this period the Indian wars continued, a constant drain upon the financial resources of the colony.

The long pastorate of Prentice's successor, Timothy Harrington, covered the stormy period of the Revolution, in which Lancaster naturally took a full part. Lancaster minutemen under Captain Houghton hurried to Lexington, and many were at Bunker Hill. Oddly enough, Harrington, perhaps known to have a lingering love for the old regime, in 1777 was put upon the "blacklist" and was summoned to appear before the town meeting. Standing up when called upon to answer, "venerable with age and respected for his virtues, and laying bare his breast, he exclaimed, 'Strike, strike here, with your daggers. I am a true friend to my country.'" As the historian says, it was "quite dramatic." Later, in connection with the Unitarian controversy, Marvin says Harrington was "a good scholar, but not an original investigator," and "had not a leading mind." During his ministry the meetinghouse was enlarged and reseated, a certain amount of money having been raised by the sale of additional seats.

In 1793 Harrington's health had begun to decline, and a colleague was appointed. Calling a minister has ever been a serious matter in New England. In August "the town voted" to set apart a day for fasting and prayer "to prepare the town for settling a colleague" for Mr. Harrington, and the committee was directed to wait on Mr. Harrington and desire him to write "to such of the neighboring ministers as he might choose, to join the town in keeping the fast, and some one to preach discourses suitable to the occasion."

After repeated meetings of committees and much serious thought and deliberation during which numerous candidates were heard, Nathaniel Thayer was called, and a meeting to prepare for the ordination was held, when Mr. Thayer was "requested to address the Throne of Grace." The meetinghouse was furbished up by some painting and whitewashing, including the "front-work of the galleries, the pulpit and the deacon's seat," and the floors and galleries strengthened for the extra weight of the congregation expected. The ordination took place at the appointed time; the sermon was printed by subscription; and "the president of the university at Cambridge" became the fortunate possessor of six copies. Last but perhaps not least, the committee of entertainment presented their bill for £57 (then amounting to about $190.00) and received a vote of thanks for "their timely and useful exertions in preparing suitable provision, etc., for the ordaining council and for the polite manner in which they conducted the business of attending upon them."

The young minister, described as "large in person" and of "imposing presence," called to the church at the age of twenty-four, was beginning a pastorate of nearly half a century. He was born in Hampton, New Hampshire, in 1769, the son of the Reverend Ebenezer Thayer, and his mother was a daughter of the Reverend John Cotton of Newton, descended through a long line of clergymen from that Reverend John Cotton of the towns of Boston of both old and New England whose daughter married Increase Mather. Thayer's descendants for several generations have been devoted benefactors of Lancaster.

If, as Marvin says, the parish had been generous to John Whiting in 1688 in presenting him with a house, they developed the true New England thrift by the time of Mr. Thayer, for their agreement with him was that he should be paid one hundred pounds "in one year from the day of his ordination, without interest, and that an obligation should be given him for the payment of the other hundred pounds of his settlement, payable in two years from the day of his ordination, with interest from that day till paid." There is little doubt that most of the New England clergy worked for their keep.

Dogs seem to have been a frequent cause of disturbance in New England meetinghouses—no doubt particularly in summer, when church doors were open. In August, 1794, the townspeople had to be *"earnestly requested* to confine their *dogs* at home, in the future, on Sundays." Churchwardens' accounts for English and Welsh and Scottish churches in the seventeenth and eighteenth centuries list payments to "expellers" of disorderly dogs —in some cases considerable amounts, indicating that the office was by no means a sinecure. The instruments of expulsion are still to be seen in a few old churches: curious tongs or forceps of oak or iron opening and shutting in the form of a lattice, some with cruel spikes or teeth. At Youlgreave, in Derbyshire, the dog whipper's pew remained until 1868.

Another source of irritation was in "those persons" who habitually "made use of the pillows in the meeting-house to hang their hats on" and had to be requested to find some other place for them.

Twenty-two years after Mr. Thayer came to Lancaster, at a town meeting held on the first of May, 1815 (note that church business was still a matter for town meeting), a committee was chosen to purchase land suitable for a new meetinghouse. For once the people seem to have been in agreement as to the site —part of Captain Benjamin Lee's farm bordering on the main street at the "Center." The committee reported that the two acres required were worth $633.33 "and no more." This apparently was satisfactory to the Captain, for the land was conveyed to "the inhabitants of the town of Lancaster" and the selectmen authorized to receive the deed, and, at the same time, it was voted "to have a clock dial." As yet no mention was made of architect or drawings, though in December an "estimate" of $14,000 for a brick building seventy-one feet square inside, with porch, tower, and cupola, was somehow obtained, in accordance with which it was voted to build. Early in January it was decided that the "house" should face south; but, as we have seen, these matters were not so lightly determined. Captain Cleveland was the only man who kept a coach, and he came to the meeting in imposing style, which prompted one facetious citizen to move that the building should face south because "Mr. Cleveland comes up the road from the south, and thus will directly approach the door." Other caustic comments followed, and the meeting was adjourned with the matter unsettled. Three months later, a committee of twelve, six each for either side, was chosen, which chose a committee of six, which chose a "locating committee," which took another two months to report in favor of the south front. But the west-siders were still unbeaten and insisted upon doors both west and south. After more debate "it was voted" that the locating committee and the committee who selected them had acted "with fairness and candor" and that "no undue influence was had on the occasion of locating the meeting-house." It was unanimous; the "gentlemen of the locating committee" were given a vote of thanks and invited to retire to Mr. Rand's tavern, "where refreshment is provided for them by the selectmen," and after sufficient refreshment to brace them for the final resolution, the question was put as to the additional entrance, with twenty for and seventy-five against. Thus were the rights and privileges of the New England democracy duly respected; rights and privileges unrelinquished in town meetings even to the present day.

The cornerstone was laid with due ceremony on the 9th of July, 1816. The date of dedication was fixed for the first of the following January, and then only, from the description of the building published at the time, do we learn that "Charles Bulfinch, Esq., of Boston," was the architect of the church.

For a time the old meetinghouse was used as a town house, though in cold weather an adjournment to the tavern "was effected"—this, no doubt, by a vote which was unanimous on the first motion.

The change in doctrinal views which came to many New England churches had begun in Lancaster in the time of Mr. Harrington. Dr. Thayer was a liberal, in sympathy with the views of Channing and Kirkland. As seems often to have been the case, the Unitarians "held the fort"; the adherents of the older doctrine were finally forced to withdraw, and in 1841 they built their own church.

Although for more than two hundred years the affairs of the New England churches continued to occupy the attention of the voters in town meeting (all males), we are told that, of the nearly four hundred persons admitted to the church during Dr. Thayer's pastorate, only about a quarter were men.

When Lafayette made his journey through New England in 1826, he spent the night at Sampson Wilder's fine house, still standing in near-by Bolton. The next morning Dr. Thayer delivered an address of welcome, standing on the common near the church, at the closing words of which Lafayette "trembled with emotion." Years later, aged men who had been present said that Dr. Thayer's voice could be heard across the intervale and halfway up the side of George Hill—at least a mile and a half away! It is said that Lafayette often afterwards referred with pleasure to the beautiful scenery of the banks of the Nashua and "the heart-thrilling address of the venerable minister of Lancaster."

Probably few New England ministers had a greater influence over town affairs than Dr. Thayer, and it was said that the selectmen did not mend a piece of road without first consulting him.

Death ended his pastorate of nearly half a century in 1840, when he was on a journey to Niagara Falls. His successor was Edmund H. Sears, who, though much liked by the people, remained only six years, his health making a smaller parish desirable; and in August, 1847, George M. Bartol, a graduate of the Harvard Divinity School, began another long pastorate of fifty years. In his ordination, Edward Everett Hale, then at the Church of the Unity in Worcester, took a part and Dr. Bartol's brother, Cyrus Bartol, preached the sermon.

Dr. Bartol was the eighth minister during the two hundred

and eighteen years of the church's history. Three of them together had covered a period of a hundred and thirty-five years. Many people of middle age or not long past today can remember him, a much-loved, venerable figure with long white hair and beard. The end of his pastorate brings this notable church and community to the beginning of the present century.

Not far away, on the road to Clinton, is the beautiful old parsonage dating from some time before 1785, first occupied by Mr. Harrington and ever since the home of the church's ministers.

We have seen some fine old towns and villages on our New England church pilgrimage. Groton is among the loveliest of all. It is a "school town" and one of its schools, at least, is wealthy and highly restricted, which accounts for much.

The First Parish Meetinghouse faces the little green on the rising ground above the elm-shaded village street. Built in 1755, it has been remodeled several times; and in 1839 it was turned about to face the street—a not uncommon practice, especially if the principal entrance and interior seating arrangements were changed.

Apparently little or nothing of the present interior was there when the church was built. The last remodeling was about thirty years ago, when the decorative panels were applied to the walls. The present slip pews with their white paneling capped with light mahogany and small spindles in the upper panels recall the spindle backs of some of the early square pews. The present pulpit is characteristic of the Church of England plan rather than of this square meetinghouse. On the walls are memorial tablets with the names of distinguished parishioners and benefactors and of its ministers—the clergy of the earlier orthodox faith carefully segregated on the west wall from those of the later and more liberal persuasion, who are on the east. John Miller, who came to Groton in 1662, was the first minister. He served for only a year. The last of the Congregationalists was Daniel Chaplin, who came in 1778 and preached here for forty-eight years. After him came Charles Robinson in 1826, when the Unitarians "took over" and the more orthodox members, as so often seems to have happened, were forced to move up the street and build their own church.

FIRST PARISH MEETINGHOUSE (1755) *Groton, Massachusetts*

Among the early ministers were Samuel Willard and Caleb Trowbridge, both afterwards presidents of Harvard College.

On the same wall with the names of these pastors of an older church is a simple marble slab to the memory of Major Joseph Moors, "A Soldier at the Siege of Louisburg in 1758, Captain of a Company from this and adjacent Towns, in Colonel Prescott's Regiment at the Battle of Bunker Hill, June 17, 1775. Honored and trusted by his Townsmen." There are said to have been more men from Groton and Pepperell at Bunker Hill than from any other town in the colonies. Here also is a tablet to the memory of Judge Samuel Dana and his wife Rebecca. On the wall at the right of the arch there is a particularly attractive memorial to Governor Boutwell, who lived in the house opposite the town hall.

Until 1859 town meetings were held in this church; and here from 1776 to 1787 sat the Court of General Sessions of the Peace and the Court of Common Pleas for Middlesex County, for Groton was then one of the shire towns of Massachusetts. The church bell was cast in Paul Revere's foundry.

In marked contrast with this little meetinghouse is the beautiful Gothic chapel of Groton School, its fine tower plainly seen above the treetops a mile or more away. This was designed by the English architect, Henry Vaughan.

Groton suffered from repeated attacks by the Indians. Destroyed during King Philip's War and abandoned, the village was rebuilt and less than twenty years later suffered another attack. Again in Queen Anne's War several of the inhabitants were killed, and three children of Thomas Tarbell carried off to Canada.

The town is on the old stage road from Boston through Keene and Bellows Falls to Hanover, New Hampshire, and the north. Just beyond the church is the fine old Groton Inn; an important stage house in early days, it is now well patronized by motorists and others who come for a longer stay.

VII

THE FIRST BAPTIST MEETINGHOUSE, PROVIDENCE, TRINITY CHURCH AT NEWPORT, AND OLD LYME IN CONNECTICUT

Both architecturally and historically, the First Baptist Meetinghouse in Providence is one of the most notable of our early New England churches, ranking with the Center Church in New Haven and the Old South in Boston. Externally, its importance is chiefly due to the fine tower and spire, one of the most elaborate in design of any of our early churches, in which it perhaps may be classed with the Center Church and Park Street in Boston. Comparison with one of the plates in Gibbs's "Book of Architecture" (published in London in 1728) makes it perfectly evident that one of the three designs in the book for the spire of St. Martin's, London, was used. Furthermore, in a copy of the book known to have been in the possession of Caleb Ormsbee, a carpenter-architect of Providence of the time of its construction, there may be seen in faint lead pencil the words "First Baptist Church, Providence," under the middle design. Though Ormsbee was the architect and builder of the second meetinghouse of the First Congregational Church in Providence, it is not known that he worked on the Baptist church. It is interesting to compare the Gibbs plate with an old engraving of the spire of the Providence church and with the actual structure, noting the way in which the architect reduced the scale of the orders and other details, to adapt them to construction in wood. One hundred and eighty-five feet high, this lasting monument and tribute to its architect and builders has withstood three hurricanes: in 1815, when it "wavered and bent to the blast, but fell not"; in 1938, when Providence was particularly hard hit and once more in September, 1944. It would be interesting to know just how it was raised.

FIRST BAPTIST MEETINGHOUSE (1775) *Providence, Rhode Island*

The design of the church and the working drawings are believed to have been made by Joseph Brown, "merchant, astronomer, philosopher," one of four famous brothers, John, Joseph, Nicholas, and Moses Brown. Joseph, a wealthy merchant and evidently an amateur architect of considerable ability, was a member—probably the chairman—of the committee of three charged with the work. He is known to have designed at least two houses still standing—for himself and his brother. John Brown supervised the work, assisted by Joseph and a large committee. Joseph Sumner of Boston was the master workman.

The church was dedicated in May, 1775, just at the outbreak of war. In spite of the ever forced and meaningless motif of the broken cornice and frieze supporting the plaster vaults over the aisles, the interior is impressive, although one cannot but regret the removal of the old square pews with their center aisle in 1832, when the original fine high pulpit and sounding board were taken out. The elaborate arrangement of platform with mahogany pulpit and screen was installed in 1884, a memorial to Nicholas Brown 2nd and Mrs. Hope Brown Ives. Originally there was an upper gallery at the west end for "slaves, freedmen and Indians," but it made way in 1834 for the organ, the gift of Nicholas Brown 2nd. Of this gallery, Dr. King in his "Historical Statement" rather naïvely remarks that it was "not so much for the purpose of isolating them as to recognize that in this notable house of worship a place for them, too, should be provided." We wonder.

It may be noted that when pledges had been secured for the originally estimated £5,000, an additional £2,000 for a larger building was raised by lottery—a common means of raising money at the time; but the historian hastens to add that this "was the first and only instance in the history of the church."

The beautiful crystal chandelier was brought from England in 1792, the gift of Hope Brown in memory of her father, the first Nicholas. It was first lighted for her marriage to Thomas Poynton Ives. Until 1884 it was lighted with candles, then by gas, and since 1914 by electricity. The various members of the Brown family have ever been generous patrons of the city of Providence and this church.

Three times daily, as of old, the bell, pride of an ever faithful sexton, rings out above the city, at sunrise, at noon, and at nine o'clock. Weighing 2,500 pounds, it was made in London, with the inscription:

> For freedom of conscience the town was first planted,
> Persuasion, not force, was used by the people:
> This Church is the eldest, and has not recanted,
> Enjoying and granting bell, temple and steeple.

Three times cracked and recast, it is now inscribed with the date of the origin of the church and the name of Roger Williams, "its first pastor, and the first asserter of liberty of conscience."

Of course the church and its history are inseparably connected with the name of Roger Williams. Founded in 1638, it is the oldest church in the state and the oldest Baptist church in America. The first settlers, under Williams's leadership, came here in 1636 after his banishment from Salem. He and his wife Mary among others were excluded from the church there "for having been rebaptized." Although it has been the popular belief that the persecution of Williams was entirely upon religious grounds, it is likely that his opinions as to the validity of the colony's charter and other civil matters may have had much to do with his banishment, and particularly his contention that, the Indians being the true owners of the land, the King had no right to grant a charter. He had proposed cutting out the cross from the flag, and when other churches failed to agree with his views he advised his church at Salem to withdraw fellowship with them, and set up a private conventicle in his own house; and when his wife continued to attend the Salem church he renounced fellowship with her and refused to say family prayers and grace at table in her presence. He was cited to appear before the magistrates and, after what seems to have been a fair trial, was ordered to be banished. The authorities, having heard that he was planning to start a colony in Narragansett, undertook to ship him back to England; but he managed to escape in the middle of January, making his way through the snow to the friendly Indians of Rhode Island.

The tradition is, that after an attempt to establish a settlement in the neighborhood of East Providence, Williams was

INTERIOR OF THE FIRST BAPTIST MEETINGHOUSE *Providence, Rhode Island*

paddling down the Seekonk River in June of 1636 when an Indian standing on a rock on the west bank hailed him with the greeting, "What cheer, friend?" Though there is a tradition that he landed here, it is thought that he kept on around Fox Point and paddled up Great Salt (Providence) River to the junction of the Woonasquatucket and Moshassuck, where, near the ever important "fresh and copious spring," he founded the settlement. Here in the wilderness the little band of twelve or more established a "new order" which they believed was in accordance with the teaching of the New Testament. Strangely, in a few months the founder withdrew from formal membership, having become convinced that, "owing to the corruption in Christendom," the rites of the Church had become invalid, and that there was no proper administrator and no proper church. He continued to live in the vicinity, working for the enlightenment and conversion of the Indians, whose confidence he had won and always retained. His labors antedated those of Eliot and are said to have been no less successful. He strove constantly and self-denyingly for the peace and prosperity of the state which he had founded, at his own expense making two visits to England in its interests. He died in 1683, and "was buried with all the solemnity the colony was able to show"; and in Rhode Island his name is venerated as that of a sort of patron saint.

After Williams's withdrawal, four ministers "held the pastoral office conjointly" for about twenty years: Chad Brown, Thomas Olney, William Wickenden, and Gregory Dexter—all men of strong character and competent leadership who left a numerous posterity to become leaders in the state.

For sixty years the little band had no church or meeting-house, holding services in the homes of the members "or under the trees." The first little church was built in 1700 by Pardon Tillinghast, the sixth minister; and he deeded it in the same year to the Baptist church. It stood at the corner of what are now North Main and Smith streets, to be succeeded in fifteen years by a larger building, forty feet square, on the same spot.

The present "house," as the grand old church is rather inadequately described in Dr. King's "Historical Statement," stands in an open space of more than an acre in the center of the city, on North Main Street. Tall commercial buildings surround it at no great distance, and a steady stream of traffic constantly passes the foot of the sloping green. Once this same green must have extended in an unbroken sweep down to the Great Salt River—now a sluggish underground canal.

James Manning was pastor during the Revolution. He was the sixth in succession to Pardon Tillinghast, whose devoted efforts had given the community the second little church; and the sixteen following him have served for periods of one to eighteen years—unaccountably short for New England pastorates.

Brown University commencements have always been held in the church in accordance with an agreement when it was built.

The crowded streets of old Newport ramble up and down the hillside between sophisticated Bellevue Avenue and the water front. Along Thames Street and the streets adjoining, there still linger among modern shop fronts many ancient wooden houses and other buildings dating from the early years of the town. Here are the beautiful brick Colony House and the Old Brick Market.

Old Trinity Church stands in its little burying ground on the steep hill of Church Street, where once a sloping stretch of greensward extended to the harbor.

"The loveliest wooden church steeple that was ever built," says a loyal Newport woman of its spire. And although lifelong residents and devoted admirers of the town may be a bit prejudiced the old church remains today both architecturally and historically a priceless survival from colonial days. Spared by the British during their occupation of Newport, it has been but little changed since it was built. From the high pulpit with its great sounding board a succession of rectors beginning with James Honeyman, have preached the gospel for more than two hundred years. Queen Anne gave the church a bell, and Bishop Berkeley, then Dean of Derry, gave the organ. The great man first arrived in Newport, in January, 1729, when Mr. Honeyman was preaching. Hastily dismissing the people, he and his entire congregation hurried down to Ferry Wharf to welcome him.

Berkeley was on his way to Bermuda, to found a college for "the Better Supplying of Churches in our Foreign Plantations,

STUDY OF THE SPIRE OF TRINITY CHURCH (1726) *Newport, Rhode Island*

DOORWAYS OF TRINITY CHURCH *Newport, Rhode Island*

and for Converting the Savage Americans to Christianity," and he waited at Newport for the arrival of the charter and a grant of twenty thousand pounds promised him by the King; but they never arrived. He lived for three years at "Whitehall," the house he built at near-by Middletown, and then returned to England. His infant daughter lies buried in Trinity churchyard.

Peter Harrison—whom we have already met in connection with King's Chapel, Boston, and Christ Church, Cambridge—and his brother Joseph lived at Newport from 1740 on. In 1776 Peter married a daughter of the younger Edward Pelham and came into possession of a good deal of Newport property (Harrison Avenue is named for him). With his brother he designed the Redwood Library; and he was the architect of the Old Brick Market and the Jewish Synagogue. He completed the beautiful Colony House after the death of Richard Munday, who designed it.

Francis Nicholson, a zealous churchman, arrived in America in 1686 and became lieutenant governor of the Dominion of New England under Andros. He visited Newport in 1694. He was instrumental in securing a Church of England clergyman for the town, and the first little building for the services was built in 1704, to be replaced twenty-two years later by the church we see today.

Mr. Honeyman died in 1750. During the next ten years there were two successive rectors, followed by Marmaduke Browne, of whose father Arthur we shall hear in Portsmouth.

Richard Munday was the designer of Trinity Church, built in 1726. The spire, rebuilt about the time the church was enlarged in 1762, is very much like the original spire of Christ Church, Boston, and very likely was intended for a copy. Opinions differ as to whether the surmounting vane is crown or miter.

Though the interior of Trinity has been likened to Christ Church, except in the arrangement of the galleries they are not very much alike. The groined ceiling, something like that of King's Chapel, suggests the influence of Wren's English churches.

As originally built, Trinity had five bays; but by 1740 the building was becoming crowded, and additional pews were built wherever possible. Even the christening pew was turned into sittings, and Captain Rouse had to be told that he must take the lock off his pew "and admit some person to sit therein, who will allow him something for it, and also contribute weekly."

In 1762 the church was lengthened. The building was cut in two, the chancel moved back to the Spring Street line, and two new bays added to the nave. By close observation, it may be noted that these are shorter than the others. As of other New England churches, it has been said that the steeple "was probably constructed from a design of Sir Christopher Wren"; but there seems to be no particular evidence of this. Part of the spire was blown off in a gale in 1731, and soon after the church was lengthened the tower and spire were rebuilt. Money for this was raised by a lottery authorized by the General Assembly —a favorite means of raising funds for church building in Rhode Island about this time.

In the soft glow of the afternoon light which filters through the time-dimmed glass of the many-paned windows, there is a charm and atmosphere about the interior of old Trinity to be found in no other of our early New England churches.

The most striking feature is the high pulpit and sounding board with clerk's desk below, at the end of the center aisle, cutting off the view from the nave of the shallow chancel and communion table or altar. The original pulpit in Christ Church, Cambridge, was in this position, and the arrangement is still to be found in at least one old church in the South. In Trinity Church there is little more than space for the single row of communicants at the altar rail.

When the restorations of 1928 were made, the modern altar which for many years had replaced the old communion table was removed and the oak table restored to its place.

The ancient pews remain unchanged, still upholstered in varying shades of red or green according to the taste of their owners. In some are armchairs for older members of the family. On the aisle at the wardens' pews are the staves of office always seen in parish churches in England. The gilt miters and royal crown still surmount the organ, the central part of which was given by Bishop Berkeley, though the royal arms at the east window were torn down and burnt during the Revolution. Upon the walls are tablets, many of them notably beautiful in design and execution, to the memory of departed members of the parish: some bearing names famous in New York and Newport society; some, names distinguished in the history of the town or the nation. One on the north wall, in memory of Sarah, wife of William Atherton, tells us that

> If an Afemblage of all the Virtues
> Which adorn and dignify
> the Soul,
> United to Elegance of Person,
> and refinement of manners,
> Could have rescued her from death;
> She still had lived.

Sarah Atherton was the daughter of the West Indian merchant Jahleel Brenton. She died in 1787 and is buried in the Clifton burying ground. There is a tablet to the memory of members of the Malbone family on the south wall. The Malbone pew was number thirty-two.

Candles in the fine old brass chandeliers are still used to light the church.

In the churchyard are the graves of Admiral de Ternay and Lafayette's aide-de-camp, the Chevalier de Fayelle.

What scenes of pomp and circumstance has the old church witnessed! In the early days of the town's commercial activity and social splendor, what an array of scarlet coats and brocade, of lace ruffles and powdered hair, must have filled these pews! But in December, 1776, a British fleet under Sir Peter Parker sailed up the Sakonnet River, and troops under General Clinton and Lord Percey took possession of the town to hold it for three years, until in July of 1780 the French fleet under De Ternay, bringing Rochambeau and five thousand men, occupied the place, and French officers, many of them distinguished members of the French nobility, brought a renewal of social activity and gayety. In March, 1781, Washington came for a conference with Rochambeau and, wearing the uniform of a marshal of France, was received with the highest military honors. The following evening a grand ball was given in honor of the two distinguished generals; the houses of the town were illuminated, and lights on the steeple of old Trinity shone far out over the harbor.

Samuel Seabury, after his consecration by the Scottish bishops in 1784 as the first Episcopal bishop in the United States, preached his first sermon here.

One of Trinity's most wealthy parishioners was Godfrey Malbone, whose son Godfrey built the little church still standing in Brooklyn, in Connecticut, which we shall see. Godfrey the elder, one of New England's first great merchants who made a fortune on the sea, built himself a fine country house at Newport, designed by Peter Harrison. Those were the days of privateering, but the deeds of Malbone's corsairs sailing out of Newport were notorious, "lawless, even for this lawless age." Tales were told of a mysterious underground passage from the house to the beach, by which cargoes could be landed free from the prying eyes of troublesome customs officers.

On the day before Christmas in 1745, two of Malbone's privateers, large and beautiful ships just off the stocks, sailed out of Newport Harbor for the West Indies, never to be heard of again. That winter Newport had two hundred widows.

Wild tales were told of princely entertainments, when returned successful buccaneers were feasted and the house rang with their songs. One day in 1766 Malbone invited the élite of the town to the most lavish entertainment of all. As the negro servants were bringing in the first course, a fire broke out; but Malbone swore that, though his house might be lost, his dinner should not. The tables were dragged out to the lawn, and the dinner went on while he and his guests watched the finest mansion in the colonies burn to the ground. Today there is a modern house upon the site—on Malbone Road, about half a mile from Broadway. His town house, on Thames Street, is now a home for aged women.

Great fortunes like Malbone's were dispersed by the Revolution, but the loss of his two ships with valuable cargoes thirty years before is said to have been the first step in the decline of his fortunes.

In later years Trinity Church was the scene of fashionable weddings, with Vanderbilts, Astors, and Goelets in leading parts; but the heyday of Newport as the fashionable summer capital has passed. Today much of the town's importance is due to the presence of the Naval War College and Naval Training Station. The spire of old Trinity still looks out across the harbor and down upon the clustering chimneys of ancient houses, and the church's staid and formal interior with its old box pews is little changed from the day when Berkeley landed and Bishop Seabury preached his first sermon in New England from its high pulpit.

At Old Lyme, that pleasant, elm-shaded village of dignified old mansions at the mouth of the Connecticut, there stands in the main street a fine church which has been justly described perhaps as "one of the most perfect early nineteenth century churches in New England."

Above the porch and pediment supported by four Ionic columns, the fine tower rises in three stages, the upper octagon with delicate engaged columns surmounted by a slender spire. Fluted columns of the Ionic order support the balconies of the auditorium, their fronts elaborately ornamented with the modilions and dentils of the order. Pilasters and entablature are carried around the wall of the elliptical "apse," with stairs and balustrade on each side leading to the pulpit, which faces a broad center aisle.

Colonel Samuel Belcher is recorded as the builder, though the favorite tradition that he followed plans of one of Wren's London churches is of course unfounded.

Probably few who do not know its history realize that this is not an old church, but a reproduction of the original building of 1816, which was destroyed by fire on the 3rd of July, 1907. (At the dedication of the present building in the summer of 1910, Woodrow Wilson, then president of Princeton, made the address.) Although the old meetinghouse certainly was unlike any English church, it is said that plans brought from England by Charles Griswold in 1814 had been preserved and were used for the reproduction.

Old Lyme and its neighbors, North, South, and East Lyme and Hadlyme, originally were parts of Saybrook and were set off as Lyme in 1665. Two families of Dutch settlers came to Saybrook as early as 1623, though when a shipload of Dutch came ten years later they had disappeared. But the first permanent settlement was about 1635, when Lord Saye and Sele, Lord Brooke, and others with an English patent sent John Winthrop, Jr., Governor Winthrop's son, as agent and governor and he named it Saybrook. Soon Dutch ships sailed into the harbor; but, finding that the English had built a fort and mounted guns, they sailed away again.

At one time it was expected that some of those who had become unpopular with the English government on account of their opposition to King Charles's tax for the so-called ship money would find a refuge here. Cromwell himself, according to Macaulay, with his cousin John Hampden in 1637 actually went on board a ship in the Thames. The ship is said to have been driven back by adverse winds, and meanwhile an order of council had been issued forbidding her to sail. Thus one of those romantic tales was frustrated: Cromwell to Saybrook, Marie Antoinette to Edgecomb, the Dauphin to Longmeadow, Napoleon to Bolton, and Marshal Ney to South Carolina.

The first settler within the area of Old Lyme was Matthew Griswold, first of that famous name in Connecticut, who sailed from Lyme Regis; that ancient seaport of historic past on the coast of Dorset. It was from Lyme Regis that the boat was to come for Charles after the battle of Worcester, while he waited at the inn at near-by Charmouth: a plan frustrated by one of those seemingly trivial and inconsequential incidents which have marred other plots before and since. The captain's wife had become suspicious, and, fearing for her husband's life if he were discovered, she locked him in his room, making safety double sure by hiding his breeches.

In 1636 Colonel George Fenwick arrived to act as governor of Saybrook until the settlement was sold to the colony of Connecticut in 1644. His first wife, the Lady Alice Boteler, was the first lady of rank to come to the colony. For nine years she shared with her husband the hardships and dangers of the early settlement; when she succumbed to them she was buried in a bleak and barren part of the Point a few yards southwest of the Saybrook fort—a spot afterwards known as Tomb Hill. Here her husband erected a monument before he returned to England, confiding her grave to the care of Matthew Griswold,

THE CONGREGATIONAL CHURCH (1910) *Old Lyme, Connecticut*

to whom he gave a grant of land across the river. For more than two hundred years the grave was undisturbed, until the line of the Connecticut Valley Railroad was laid out directly through it. On opening the grave the lady's bright golden hair was found perfectly preserved; part of it was kept by a conductor on the railroad. In the village cemetery where she now lies the moss-grown slab bears simply her name, "Lady Fenwick," and the date.

On his return to England Fenwick served in the Long Parliament and was appointed a member of the High Court of Justice to try Charles I, though he did not serve. He had been a colonel in the parliamentary army and was successively governor of Tynemouth, Berwick, and Edinburgh and Leith.

The church burnt in 1907 was the fourth. The first was at Black Hall on the old Post Road, and it was followed by two others "more commodious and substantial," in 1689 and 1734, on near-by sites. In 1815 the third was struck by lightning and burnt, having once before narrowly escaped burning when some zealous person set it on fire with his gun wadding in attempting to get rid of a flock of woodpeckers, thought to be seriously damaging the roof. Hessian soldiers then quartered in the town climbed upon the roof and put out the fire. By the early part of the nineteenth century the town had grown up farther inland, and in 1816 the fourth, prototype of the present church, was built on the main street at the corner of Ferry Road. Until 1850 this was allowed to keep its high pulpit and old square pews; but then, like so many others, it succumbed to the popular innovations of the time and they were removed.

Moses Noyes was the minister of the first little church built at Black Hall. He had one of those long pastorates of over fifty years, not infrequent in New England, and was followed by Samuel Pierpont—early ancestor of the noted Connecticut family—whose pastorate was tragically brief. A few months after coming to the town he was crossing the Connecticut to Essex to visit a young woman with whom he was enamored, when his canoe overturned and he was drowned. The unfortunate young man's successor was John Parsons, who married Phoebe Griswold, one of the eight famous Griswold daughters known as the "Black Hall Boys." Evidently Phoebe was not possessed of that demure character of piety usually attributed to the wife of a Puritan divine, for she is said to have been fond of practical jokes even to the extent of practicing them upon her clerical husband; and some remarkable pranks are related of this seemingly ill suited consort.

There was a time when "a sea captain once lived in every house" and graceful clipper ships slid down the ways of the Lieutenant River to sail for ports throughout the world. Two governors, Roger and Matthew Griswold, were born here; a chief justice of the United States and one of Connecticut; a justice of the United States Circuit Court, and a minister to Austria. For many years the town has been noted as a summer community of distinguished artists whose cottages and studios are along the road overlooking the Lieutenant River or elsewhere throughout the village.

Down by the waterside the old white ferry buildings are still standing, near the site of the first public ferry of 1662. Here Washington crossed in April, 1776, and here, more than a hundred years before, the first canoes had come across from Saybrook and the first settlers landed.

Killingworth has an old meetinghouse of interest and is a pleasant rural village, so we may as well follow the road, less traveled than the shore route, through to New Haven. Although the guide book tells us that the church "owes something, obviously, to Hoadley's United Church in New Haven," more obviously it is one of the many inspired by Asher Benjamin's "Design for a Church," of which we saw the first at Wayland, and which we shall come across a number of times again.

VIII

NEW HAVEN, HARTFORD, AND SOME OTHER OLD CONNECTICUT CHURCHES

It may perhaps be generally conceded that Boston's Old South holds first place among old New England meetinghouses in its historical associations, with King's Chapel and Christ Church of scarcely less importance. And in architectural interest and charm the interior of no other of our old meetinghouses or churches can quite equal the interior of the Chapel. But while we find much to admire in many of the less sophisticated old white meetinghouses the two churches on the Green at New Haven (the Center Church and the "United"—particularly the Center Church), in their exteriors perhaps are the tours de force among them all. Rather oddly, they were built at the same time, in the years from 1812 to 1815.

Although above the brick of the first stage of the tower of the Center Church the spire is of wood, we may concede that here the architect may have been inspired by that often cited spire of St. Martin-in-the-Fields of James Gibbs, though it might equally well have originated with the design in his "Book of Architecture" which seems to have given a spire to the church in Providence. The one criticism of the exterior might be of the portico, which is somewhat broad in proportion to its height.

This church is one more instance of the obscurity which has so often surrounded the architects of many of these early New England buildings. One of the most notable of the period, the Center Church has long been ascribed to Ithiel Town. Yet a report of the building committee among the church records makes clear that he was merely the builder, and not the author of the design.

Town had studied in Boston under Asher Benjamin. Later

he became associated with Captain Isaac Damon, an architect and engineer "of considerable note" in Northampton, who it appears also took building contracts—a practice now generally considered rather unethical. The contract for building the church was awarded to Damon, with the stipulation that Town should serve as his assistant. For some unknown reason, Town assumed full charge soon after the work was started, and carried it to completion. The spire was built and raised inside the brick tower.

Town designed and built Trinity Church, adjoining on the Green, one of the early examples of the Gothic revival in this country; a creditable piece of work for the time and evidence of his good taste and versatility.

Careful repairs and restorations of the exterior of the Center Church were made in 1912, when the paint was removed from the brickwork, restoring it to its condition previous to 1845.

The interior has galleries on three sides and a plaster vaulted ceiling. As yet the long projected interior restorations have not been made. The platform, the paneling and arch motif, and the much admired Davenport window are of course modern and unfortunately out of keeping with the original work of the period, as are the reading desk and other platform furniture.

On the walls are tablets to the memory of John Davenport and other early ministers and distinguished laymen of the church. In the vestibule are a memorial to Ithiel Town and a portrait of him on an adjoining wall; in this case, it seems, honor to whom honor is only partially due.

There are eight old silver chalices and a christening basin belonging to the church. Probably the earliest of these was that marked, "Given by Mr. Jno. Potter to N. haven chh." Potter is known to have been among those at the first meeting of the settlers in "Mr. Newman's barn" in 1639. One of the cups was long supposed to have been brought by John Davenport, the first minister, in the *Hector;* but the mark "I. D." in an oval or heart on this and five other pieces was the mark of John Dixwell, the regicide's son, who was a silversmith in Boston.

There is a curious romance about the christening basin. Sometime in the eighteenth century Jeremiah Atwater, wanting to repair his house, bought a keg of nails of a Boston dealer. On opening it, besides the nails he found a quantity of silver dollars.

CENTER CHURCH AND THE GREEN *New Haven, Connecticut*

FAÇADE OF CENTER CHURCH (1812–14) *New Haven, Connecticut*

CENTER CHURCH IN MARCH *New Haven, Connecticut*

Jeremiah had the Connecticut variety of New England conscience, and he tried to return the dollars to the man from whom he bought the nails. But he in turn disclaimed a right to them, and the dollars remained unclaimed. On his death, Atwater left them to the church, and from them the christening basin was made—twelve inches in diameter and more than two pounds in weight. One would like to know the true mystery of the hoard, never to be solved.

At the time of the British raid on New Haven, the church silver was in the care of Deacon Ball, who hid it in his chimney; the Deacon's little girl, it is said, being lifted up to reach the shelflike resting place.

The crypt beneath the church covers part of the old burying ground, used from the time of the first settlement in 1638 until 1813. The oldest stone, dated 1687, marks the grave of Mrs. Sarah Trowbridge. Here are buried Nicholas Street, the second minister; the Reverend James Pierpont and his third wife, a granddaughter of Thomas Hooker; Mrs. Margaret Arnold, the first wife of Benedict Arnold; and the stamp agent Jared Ingersoll. The last burial was in 1812. In 1821 the part of the ground outside the church walls was leveled off and the monuments removed to the Grove Street Cemetery.

In the old burying ground at the back of the church, enclosed by an iron railing, is the grave of the regicide John Dixwell, who lived in New Haven for many years under the name of James Davids. On the rear wall of the church are tablets to the memory of the other regicides who found sanctuary here; Cromwell's cousin Edward Whalley, and William Goffe. Though the long inscriptions describe each with his customary designation as (major) general, the name at the top of each tablet is prefixed by "Col." Both found a refuge for a time in the cave on West Rock, the cliff rising above the city in the northwest. Here also on the wall of the church is a tablet in memory of Theophilus Eaton, first governor of New Haven Colony, who is buried outside the pulpit window.

The first little meetinghouse, where in 1640 the people were called by the beating of a drum, stood a few yards in front of the present building. It was to the second, built thirty years later, that the mysterious James Davids came, for many years finding a refuge in New Haven and only after his death known to have been John Dixwell, one of the judges who tried King Charles. This second building stood for nearly ninety years. The third, known as the "brick meetinghouse," built in 1757, was demolished to give place to the fine church we see today. And so for more than three hundred years there has been continuous public worship on this spot. Here, extending to College Street, was the first burying ground.

Religious differences seem to have been a cause of much dissension in the New Haven and Connecticut colonies for the first century and a half of their existence. At the time of the arrival of the first settlers the Antinomian controversy was at its height—"a theological doctrine," says James Tueslow Adams, "which has often been considered so baffling as to elude understanding." Even at the time, Winthrop wrote of the "Covenant of Grace" and the "Covenant of Works" that "no man could tell (except some few, who knew the bottom of the matter) where any difference was." One would think that for much of the first hundred years, when they were not harrying the Indians or being harried by them, they were harrying each other. There is a story of an early settler who had spent a long evening in theological discussion with a neighbor. Picking up his gun as he stepped out into the darkness, he carefully examined the priming. "What is the use of that?" asked his friend. "If it is foreordained that an Indian should kill you, you cannot help yourself." "True," said the other, "but if it is foreordained that I should kill an Indian, I must be ready."

John Davenport and Theophilus Eaton headed a party of English settlers here in 1637–38. "In accordance with custom" they bought the land from the Indians. The price paid for the area now included in New Haven and North Haven and the towns of Wallingford, Cheshire, Bethany, Orange, and other land adjoining consisted of twenty-three coats, two dozen knives and a dozen spoons, a dozen hatchets and some hoes, scissors, and porringers.

Davenport (otherwise Damport or Dampard), an Oxford man, had been curate of St. Lawrence, Jewry—the old Gothic church destroyed in the great fire of 1666, predecessor of Wren's now of the noble company of his London churches as far from us today as Davenport's. St. Stephen's Coleman Street, of which he was vicar, is still standing.

Theophilus Eaton, son of a Coventry minister, had been a London merchant of wealth and prominence and had served in some capacity at the Danish court.

The company was a distinguished one, including several other London merchants besides Eaton; five ministers; three school-teachers; and the father of Elihu Yale. They arrived in the early summer, "just in time to take part in the Antinomian controversy and the taxes for the Pequot War. Mr. Davenport was requested to contribute to the former, and Mr. Eaton to the latter." Eaton and Davenport had been for some years members of the Massachusetts Bay Company. They can have wasted little time in apportioning the land and getting to work on their buildings; for we are told that in June of the following year—1639—they met in "Newman's barn" and elected Eaton magistrate; he was not called governor until the colony was more fully organized in 1643. They voted to be governed by the rules of Scripture in all things, both church and state. The "free burgesses"—church members—chose the twelve electors, among them Eaton, Davenport, Newman, and Richard Malbon, who in turn chose the "seven pillars" to establish a church. They called the colony by the Indian name, Quinnipiac, for the first two years, when it was changed to Newhaven, after the town on the English Channel, on the coast of Sussex.

Davenport is supposed to have first preached under an oak which stood near their landing place. The first meetinghouse was built on the common—the present Green—in the year after their arrival. With Davenport for twelve years as "teacher" was William Hooke, friend and chaplain of Oliver Cromwell. His wife was the Protector's cousin and Whalley's sister. Returning to England, ("Old England, dear England" as he said, "never yet forsaken in our affections"), he became domestic chaplain to Cromwell in his palace of Whitehall and Master of the Savoy Hospital. But after a few years the Commonwealth became a thing of the past and Hooke spent the rest of his life in more or less danger, "resting at last in Bunhill Fields, the 'Westminster Abbey of the Puritans.'" His parting gift to the little church in New Haven had been his "home lot" on the southwest corner of College and

Chapel streets, "to be a standing maintenance either towards a teaching office, schoolmaster, or the benefit of the poor in fellowship." This is said to have been one of the inducements which influenced the college in the choice of New Haven. The church finally leased it to the college for 999 years. It was Davenport's plan that the "rector's house" should be here; and here all the rectors and presidents of Yale lived from Cutler to the elder Dwight.

The church's second teacher was Nicholas Street, the third Oxonian. For six years after Davenport went to Boston, to the Old South, Street served as pastor, though he never was regularly installed. James Pierpont, Harvard graduate and first American-born pastor, was settled in 1684. Among the first of that famous name in Connecticut, he was one of the memorable ten who contributed from their own scanty stock of books to found the college, and it is said to have been on account of his efforts with Jeremiah Dummer, Connecticut agent in London, that Elihu Yale made his gift. There is a pathetic story of Pierpont's young wife, a granddaughter of John Davenport: that in accordance with the custom of the time she went to church on her first Sunday, a cold November day, in her wedding gown, caught cold and died within three months. But it was not expected that the minister should remain long unmarried, and in two years he married Sarah, a granddaughter of Governor Haynes of Connecticut Colony. She too died after a little more than two years. But his third and last, a granddaughter of the Reverend Thomas Hooker, survived him many years. Their daughter, Sarah, married the great Jonathan Edwards. Thus James Pierpont was the ancestor of the younger Jonathan Edwards, president of Union College, and three presidents of Yale—the two Timothy Dwights and Theodore Woolsey. It is Sarah who is buried in the crypt beneath the church.

During the pastorate of Pierpont's successor Joseph Noyes, the controversies arose which led to the establishment of both the second church and the Church of England.

It was said that the New Haven Colony produced more theologians than all the rest of the country. Their theology, as we have found in others of the colonies, was mostly of that contentious variety which brooked no dissent from the opinions of established authority, and they would go to any length to enforce them. Only in 1705 was the law against "Heretics, Infidels and Quakers" annulled. To the New Lights the Old Lights were "Hirelings, caterpillars, Pharisees, Seed of the Serpent, dead dogs." Yet some of them occasionally met together in the interests of harmony, and Josiah Dwight of Woodstock prayed that they "might so hitch their horses together on earth that they should never kick in the stables of everlasting salvation." One pastor, charged with a lack of orthodoxy, was asked, "Sir, don't you think that a child brings sin enough into the world with it to damn it forever?"

No detail of personal conduct or habit was too trivial or inconsequent to arouse the ire of these early "saints." In 1738 Timothy Hutchinson was required to make humble confession of sin for smiling in church. Though there were rules against drunkenness, which from what we read of the customs of the times must have been a common failing, this seems to have been the one thing which met with leniency. In the earliest days of the colony, John Jenner, being accused, was acquitted, "itt appearing to be of infirmyty and occasioned by the extremyty of the colde" —as indeed it may well have been. As late as 1790, Dr. Nathan Strong, a fellow of Yale College, chaplain of Colonel Samuel Wylly's regiment in the Revolution and pastor of the first church in Hartford, carried on a distillery in partnership with his Brother-in-law, within four hundred yards of the church. It was said that the pastor of West Hartford raised the rye which Strong distilled into whisky which the minister at East Hartford drank.

In 1734 Jonathan Edwards preached his sermons in the church at Northampton which started the Great Awakening. Setting forth the eternity of hell's torments, in July, 1741, he preached from the text "Their foot shall slide in due time," and described God as holding the sinner over hell forever "as one holds a spider over the fire." The younger Edwards, who came to New Haven in 1769, was pastor of the United Church for twenty-five years.

In 1740 George Whitefield, then twenty-six years old, reached Middletown, Connecticut, on his tour of the colonies, when Nathan Cole of Kingston was moved to a long description of his preaching:

"Now it pleased god to send mr. whitfield into this land &

. . . i longed to see & hear him . . . & then one morning all on a Suding there came a messenger & said mr. whitfield . . . is to preach at middletown this morning at 10 o clock i was in my field at work i dropt my tool that i had in my hand & run home and throu my house & bad my wife get ready quick to go and hear mr. whitfield preach at middletown & run to my pasture for my hors with all my might fearing i should be too late to hear him . . . & took up my wife & went forward as fast as i thought ye hors could bear, & when my hors began to be out of breath i would get down & put my wife on ye saddel & bid her ride as fast as she could & not Stop or Slak for me except i bad her & so i woould run until i was almost out of breth & then mount my hors again . . . fearing we should be too late to hear ye Sarmon for we had twelve miles to ride dubble in little more than an hour."

What could be more expressive of Nathan's haste to get there? He pauses neither for breath nor for a comma. Would that we, in our times, had a modern Whitefield who could move us to such haste! He goes on:

"i saw before me a cloud or fog rising i first thought of from ye great river but as i came nearer ye road i heard a noise something like a low rumbling thunder & i presently found it was ye rumbling of horses feet coming down ye road & this Cloud was a Cloud of dust made by the running of horses feet it arose some rods into ye air over the tops of ye hills and trees & when i came within about twenty rods of ye road i could see men and horses Sliping along . . . it was like a stedy streem of horses & their riders scarcely a horse more than his length behind another . . . i found a vacance between two horses to Slip in my hors & my wife said law our cloaths will be all spoiled see how they look . . . & when we gat down to ye old meating house thare was a great multitude it was said to be 3 or 4000." And when he looked towards "ye great river" he saw the "fery boats running swift forward & backward . . . when i see mr. whitfield come up upon ye Scaffil he looked almost angellical a young slim slender youth."

In the last years of the eighteenth century there was rising opposition to Yale control in the state. In 1802 John Wood wrote: "this State has not formed any constitution since the Revolution, but ancient superstition and the prejudice of custom have established a hierarchy, which is directed by a soverign pontiff, twelve cardinals, a civil council of nine and about four hundred parochial bishops. The present priest, who may be honored with the appellation of pope, is Timothy Dwight, President of Yale College." There was still no epithet with which to damn opponents equal to Roman hierarchy and the Scarlet Woman.

Although for obvious reasons the Church of England always met with violent opposition in New England, its supporters had rather more success in establishing churches in Connecticut than in the other New England colonies. Connecticut churchmen admitted that they suffered less from persecution than those of New York and other colonies. There was an effort to establish a church at Stratford in 1707, though no parish was regularly organized for ninety years. As early as 1668 Archbishop Laud had considered the appointment of a New England bishop, and the effort for an Apostolic Episcopate did not cease until success was achieved with the consecration of Samuel Seabury as Bishop of Connecticut in 1784. Town, about the time he was building the Center Church on the Green, designed and built Trinity Church adjoining, for the Episcopalians.

New Haven suffered much during the Revolution, particularly in Tryon's attack in July, 1779, when it owed its escape from burning probably to the number of Loyalists in the place. With the hastily gathered militia was Naphtali Daggett, then college preacher. When the others took to their heels, the parson calmly stood his ground, loading and firing his shotgun. When he was wounded and the British captured him, the officer in command asked, "What are you doing here, you old fool?" "When," said the old doctor afterwards, "I failed in some degree through faintness, he would strike me on the back with a heavy walking-staff, and kick me behind with his foot."

Until 1895 all Yale commencements and other ceremonies were held in the Center Church, and for nearly a century and three-quarters successive classes have marched to take their places here and in this building's predecessors. Until 1868 proud parents and admiring friends sat through two long sessions in a day. In 1781, following the Greek oration, an English coloquy and a forensic disputation, the learned and indefatigable President Stiles in his oration delivered his opinions in Hebrew, Chaldaic, and Arabic, followed by an oration in English; all in the morning. In the afternoon he delivered a Latin discourse, when a "syllogistic dispute," a dissertation, a poem, and another oration gave the finishing touches to these learned feats. We are not surprised to hear that the younger members of the audience whispered so continuously through most of it that in course of time the sexes had to be separated and seated on opposite sides of the church.

In 1730 opposing participants in the syllogistic disputes faced each other from opposite side galleries; the audience "huddled below them to catch their Latin eloquence as it fell." In 1787 these forensic battles were given up. They had continued for sixty years—such is the power of human endurance when faced by established precedent; but as late as 1868 there were two sessions in one day and in 1857 twenty-three speakers in the morning and nineteen in the afternoon.

In the scale and refinement of detail and the general character of its architecture, the United Church on the New Haven Green, designed by David Hoadley, is more typical of New England work of the period than Damon's, and the proportions of the portico are better. The upper part of the tower is so like Bulfinch's church at Lancaster (the Lancaster church was built about a year later) that one wonders which inspired the other, or whether both came from some common source. Certainly Bulfinch was fond of this cupola motif. His Hartford State House was built in 1796, though the cupola, much like that of the old New York City Hall, was not added until 1827.

The elaborate domed and coffered ceiling was something of an innovation in Connecticut churches. We must regret that the interior, like so many others, has been reconstructed. The "alcove," with its heavy pilasters supporting the ornate cornice and too flat ellipse, was built in 1850, and at this time the galleries were lowered, and the present pulpit in the taste of the time substituted for the fine mahogany high pulpit on six fluted columns eight feet tall. Two of the three fine crystal chandeliers, made in France, were sold, when the candle sockets of the third and larger one were removed and it was fitted for gas. Fortunately, through the influence of Dr. Munger, who in 1885 became pastor, stained glass, wholly inappropriate in churches of this period,

UNITED CHURCH (1813–15) *New Haven, Connecticut*

has not been installed. On the walls there are tablets to the memory of the architect, Hoadley; Roger Sherman, one of the signers of the Declaration of Independence and first mayor of New Haven; governors of the state and others of eminence connected with the church.

Here, in 1855, Henry Ward Beecher preached to the party of eighty antislavery men who were leaving to join John Brown in Kansas, provided with rifles and Bibles from funds contributed by the congregation.

As we have seen, the preaching of the elder Jonathan Edwards, followed by the religious frenzy caused by Whitefield's visit ten years later, had started the revival movement of the Great Awakening. In 1742, taking advantage of the Act of Toleration, the New Lights appealed to the court and succeeded in establishing a "Separate" Church. In 1744 they built the "Blue Meeting-House," so called apparently on account of the color of the interior. This stood at the corner of Church and Elm streets.

Samuel Bird was the first minister. Bird had been a student at Harvard, but did not graduate. He came from Dunstable, Massachusetts, in 1751 and remained as pastor for seventeen years, when he was "dismissed" on account of ill health. During that time, in 1755, he served as chaplain in the French and Indian War. In 1769, he was succeeded by Jonathan Edwards the younger, son of the famous minister of Northampton.

The New Light members of the First Church having become more numerous than the Old Lights, in 1759 they organized a church for some reason unknown called the "White Haven Society."

During the ministry of the younger Edwards, "aggrieved and uneasy" over his doctrines and "dry metaphysical preaching," a group seceded and formed another church, also with an unaccountable name,—the "Fair Haven Society." The two churches joined in 1796, and became the "United Society" in 1815, when their properties were combined.

Twelve years before, the new society had given impetus to the movement to be consummated a quarter of a century later in the complete separation of church and state and the curtailing of the political power of the clergy. Abraham Bishop, son of a deacon of the church, had been invited to deliver the annual Phi Beta

Kappa oration at the Yale commencement of 1800. Instead of the learned discourse expected on this occasion, Bishop prepared a "political campaign document." Apparently the college authorities learned of the nature of this beforehand, for they refused to permit him to deliver it. It was, however, given in the Blue Meeting-House before a large audience.

By 1812, both the Blue Meeting-House and the church which the Fair Haven Society had built on the Green were in a "decayed condition" and it was decided to build a new meetinghouse—the "North Church on the Green," now known as the "United"; and twenty "respectable public spirited" members of the society were chosen for the building committee. Lumber was brought from Middletown down the Connecticut River and along the Sound without interference from the British blockading squadron off the coast when its commanding officer learned that it was for a church.

It will be worth while to leave the main road from New Haven at Beckley, in order to see the old church at historic Wethersfield on the outskirts of Hartford. Although the building was damaged by the injudicious remodeling of sixty years ago, when the tall stained-glass windows were put in and other work of doubtful merit was done, the exterior, with its walls of diamond pattern brickwork still retains much of its original charm and beauty. The spire is one of several strikingly similar in design closely resembling Trinity Church at Newport and the original spire of Christ Church, Boston. After the Lancaster massacre, Joseph Rowlandson was settled here for a pastorate of two years, until his death in 1678.

Historically, the Center Congregational Church at Hartford, the oldest church organized in the state, is of much interest, though from an architectural point of view it compares unfavorably with the churches on the Green at New Haven. Built in 1807, a few years before the New Haven churches, it suggests the beginning of the decadent period in New England architecture. The mass of the tall and overornate steeple, with its multiplicity of superimposed orders, seems too heavy for the building below it, and the parts of the various stages are poorly related. One feels that the architect let himself go and put into it about everything that he knew.

Back of the church, on Gold Street, is the old burying ground, the oldest in Hartford, dating from 1640. Here are the graves of Thomas Hooker and Samuel Stone, those pioneers who came to Hartford over the Connecticut Path, and many of the early governors of the colony.

The Dutch tried to take possession in the region of Hartford in 1633, when Governor Van Twiller of New Amsterdam sent Jacob Van Corlear who landed at the point on the river now known as Dutch Point. The same year John Oldham and his three companions came over the Connecticut Path. John Steel and some sixty families from Cambridge came in 1635, to be followed the next year by Hooker and Stone with their party, some hundred in all, driving their cattle. Hooker, a fellow of Emmanuel College, Cambridge, had preached at Chelmsford in Essex, later keeping a school where John Eliot was his assistant. Driven out by Archbishop Laud, he came to Cambridge in New England in 1633, when he was ordained as the first minister. In 1636 he was installed as the first pastor of the church at Hartford.

"Preacher, Founder, Democrat," as George Leon Walker apostrophized him, Hooker preached a sermon before the Connecticut General Court of April, 1638, for which he has been hailed as the guiding influence in the framing not only of the Connecticut constitution, but of the government of the United States. "It was the first written Constitution known to history that created a government," wrote John Fiske, "and it marked the beginnings of American democracy."

Stone also had been at Cambridge in the Bay Colony. He was born in Hertford, England, for which Hartford was named, and was a graduate of Emmanuel College, ordained but later suspended for nonconformity. Like Hooker, he had been in Essex, which, with the adjoining parts of East Anglia, sent New England so many settlers. Hooker and Stone were associated as preacher and teacher, a practice which prevailed in Connecticut for a while, though the precise functions of each are not always entirely clear.

It was partly due to the disagreement over a successor to Hooker on his death in 1647 that the dispute as to the Halfway

CENTER CONGREGATIONAL CHURCH (1807) *Hartford, Connecticut*

Covenant arose which continued to grow in violence until the time of Stone's death sixteen years later. Meanwhile the older leaders had been succeeded by two young men, John Whiting and Joseph Haynes. Whiting, who came to Hartford in 1660 from Salem, was a graduate of Harvard College. He afterwards became the first pastor of the Second Church. Haynes, a son of Governor John Haynes, came from Wethersfield.

It was in 1687, during the pastorate at the First Church of Timothy Woodbridge (a son of that John Woodbridge whom we shall later find at Newbury, Massachusetts), that Andros arrived in New England as governor and, coming to Hartford, tried to take away the Connecticut charter; this led to the famous incident of its hiding in the Charter Oak.

Both Farmington, eight miles from Hartford, and Litchfield, twenty miles farther on the same road, have notable churches. The Farmington spire is one of a number plainly indicating the influence that the Old South in Boston had throughout New England. The galleries remain, and the building is still a meeting-house in plan, but the old pews and the fine carved high pulpit with its sounding board are gone—removed in 1836. Captain Judah Woodruff of Farmington, said to have been among the best of the good builders of the eighteenth century, designed and built the church in 1771 and he, it is said, carved the pulpit capitals and vine ornament of the sounding board with great skill.

The church at Litchfield is one of several practically identical designs in adjacent localities. Thought to have been designed by Levi Newell of Southington, the Litchfield church resembles Hoadley's design at Milford and the church at Cheshire. In 1873, it was replaced by a "modern" building in the wooden Gothic taste of that time and was moved away to be used for a public hall. Now, thanks to funds privately raised, it has been returned to its original site, with the original well proportioned interior, barrel-vaulted ceiling, and mahogany high pulpit restored.

Fifteen years before the Revolution, there came to settle in Brooklyn, then part of Pomfret, a young Royalist student fresh from Oxford. He was a son of that Godfrey Malbone whom we found in Newport as a man of wealth. The father's business reverses and misfortunes necessitated the recall of the younger Godfrey to America, and he was sent to the royal manor of Kingswood in the Connecticut wilderness (bought by the elder Malbone from Governor Belcher of Massachusetts) to manage the estate, with forty slaves. Here he settled down in a small house.

Kingswood with the adjoining manor farm of Wiltshire had formed the larger manor of Mortlake, originally granted to Sir John Blackwell, an officer in Cromwell's army, as a refuge for Irish dissenters. The Restoration probably interfered with that, and the whole had been purchased by Governor Belcher, who sold the Wiltshire part to the elder Malbone's friend Major Israel Putnam.

The nearest English church was twenty miles away at Norwich; but despite the distance young Godfrey and his wife attended services as often as the weather and the state of the roads permitted. He had been in Pomfret about eight years when the Congregationalists decided to build a new meetinghouse; and, as presumably the richest man in the community, much to his indignation, he had to pay by far the greatest share of the taxes to meet the cost. Whereupon he determined to establish and build a church of the Anglican communion, and appealed to friends in England for help. For the first two or three years services were held in an old house, remains of which not long ago might still be seen. His friend the Bishop of London sent prayer books.

Timber had to be felled for the new church, and hewn with an adz or sawed, perhaps by hand, in the nearest saw pit. The frame was raised and pinned together with wooden pegs, even the nails being hammered out by hand on the blacksmith's anvil. The glass for the windows was brought from England—the Pitkin glassworks at near-by Manchester probably were not yet in full operation. Three years later, in 1771, the little church was ready for service.

Pomfret, Killingly, Plainfield, and Canterbury all were included in the parish. It took faith and zeal to bring people to church in those days—by unbroken roads where the snow lay in drifts over the high, wind-swept ridges of the Connecticut hills. For years the only heat came from the little charcoal foot warmers

THE CONGREGATIONAL CHURCH (1761) *Wethersfield, Connecticut*

THE CONGREGATIONAL CHURCH (1771) *Farmington, Connecticut*

which they brought with them, perhaps filled with coals from the nearest house, for we know from the records that it was a quarter of a century before the chimney was built.

The first rector was Mr. Moseley. His stay was brief, and he was succeeded by Daniel Fogg, who came from a parish in North Carolina. As there was no rectory Colonel Malbone took him into his own household, and found him indispensable in the declining health of his later years. Mr. Fogg stayed on after the Colonel's death, giving up his own plans to look after the business of the estate in addition to the work of the large parish. At the age of fifty he married a niece of Colonel Malbone, moving to a house which he built for himself about half a mile away.

All through his life as rector Mr. Fogg kept a diary, so that the records of his years at Brooklyn are authentic. He made repeated efforts to raise a permanent endowment for his parish, and believed that he had done so; but after his death the pledges were not paid, people saying that they made them only to ease the old gentleman's mind, and could not fulfill them!

Mr. Fogg's successor seems to have been appointed on the strength of his reputation as a preacher. People flocked to hear him and the church was filled, until it was dicovered that his fine sermons were those of various prominent English churchmen. He quarreled with his senior warden, Colonel Daniel Putnam (a son of Israel), who had married Godfrey Malbone's daughter. Yet if stories told of him are true he must have been a chicken-hearted soul, and strangely ungallant. One night, when a lady parishioner left the rectory after dark, he refused to see her home for fear of passing the churchyard alone!

Some time previous to 1825, the parish acquired a glebe of about twenty acres with an old house to be used as a rectory, and this was first occupied by Ezra Kellogg. Mr. Kellogg remained for seven years, saying at the end of that time that a minister should leave before his people got tired of him.

For about eighty years the little church stood as Godfrey Malbone had built it. Then came one of those ambitious and energetic rectors whose activities so often have been directed toward "modernizing" and improving. For some reason or other Mr. Camp had half the old windows removed. The old pulpit was pulled to pieces to make the two desks, and the sounding board

THE CONGREGATIONAL CHURCH (1828–29) *Litchfield, Connecticut*

OLD TRINITY CHURCH (1771) *Brooklyn, Connecticut*

FRONT ELEVATION OF OLD TRINITY CHURCH *Brooklyn, Connecticut*

taken down, presumably to be broken up. Fortunately the old pews with their doors were allowed to remain. Not satisfied with this, some time during his incumbency of thirty-seven years Mr. Camp decided that a new church should be built in the village, a mile and a half away; and since then, except for an evening service in summer, the little church which Godfrey Malbone built has been used only on rare occasions for special services. Once a year on All Saints' Day, it is used at the reunion of descendants of the Malbone and Putnam families.

For some sixty years, succeeding rectors occupied the stone rectory next the new church in the village; but now this is served by the rector of the church in Danielson.

Today, though altered as we have seen, Godfrey Malbone's little church still stands much as he built it. Most of the ancient oaks which once surrounded it are gone. Round about in the burying ground are the slate stones of generations of parishioners. Here, too, lie seven of its faithful and devoted rectors, the earlier ones in life not always overwelcome in this New England community.

IX

JAFFREY, PETERBOROUGH, HANCOCK, AND FITZWILLIAM—BENNINGTON, VERMONT

THERE IS ample evidence that, despite their lives of almost endless toil, our early ancestors were by no means unmindful of the attractions of a sightly location—witness many a hilltop village and scores of old farms reaching up from rough pastures on Vermont and New Hampshire mountain sides.

On such a hilltop is the village of Jaffrey, straggling down the slope to the foot of the hill. The great white meetinghouse stands at the top, facing west across the valley towards the rocky summit of Monadnock; but, sad to relate, for more than a hundred years it has been used only for a town hall. The bell is still rung to call the villagers to service in the present church, for the old steeple, more fortunate than many others throughout New England, has weathered at least two hurricanes.

Jaffrey and Dublin were in the southwestern part of the Masonian Grant of 1629, which extended to the Maine border. This was purchased in 1746 from Captain Mason's descendant, Lieutenant John Mason, by Governor Benning Wentworth and others, mostly of Portsmouth. Their charter was granted three years later, and for more than a hundred and fifty years title to portions of this grant lying on the summit and adjacent parts of the mountain had never passed from the original owners. In 1902, quitclaim deeds from seventy-seven heirs of the Masonian Proprietors were given to the Society for the Protection of New Hampshire Forests.

The earliest attempt at settlement in Jaffrey is said to have been in 1752, by nine men on the shore of Gilmore Pond. Rumors of Indians in the neighborhood soon frightened them away, but five years later John Grout of Sudbury and John Davidson purchased one of the abandoned claims. Others followed, and in 1773 an act of incorporation was granted by Governor John Wentworth in the name of King George III. The town took its name from George Jaffrey, one of the Masonian Proprietors, sometime Chief Justice of the Supreme Court of the Province of New Hampshire, member of the Governor's Council and Treasurer. A photographic copy of Copley's portrait of him hangs in the old church.

Many of the Jaffrey settlers, sons of Worcester and Middlesex County farmers, had been in the Revolutionary army. From early days until about the time of the Civil War, sheep raising and the pasturing of cattle were the great industries. As late as the first part of the nineteenth century, both wolves and bears made constant depredations upon the flocks. One farmer lost sixteen sheep in a single night. The pastures ran far up the steep slopes of the mountain. Their old stone walls are still plain to be seen, though the fields long ago grew up with the hardwood and spruce that now cover the mountain side. What weeks of toil went to the building of such walls, throughout New England, abandoned at last!

> What years of iron labor! and for what?
> To yield the chipmunk one more secret nook,
> The gliding snake one more sequestered spot.*

Yet their builders were a long-lived and prolific lot. Ages of from eighty to ninety are to be found on the records, and some lived on into the tenth decade—hardy survivors in families which had numbered from six to twelve children.

Although the terms of the Jaffrey grant by the successors of the Masonian Proprietors required that a "good, convenient meeting-house" be built within six years of the date of the charter and a provision was made for that purpose by a gift of three hundred acres of land, none had been built up to the incorporation of the town in 1773. The following year, however, it was voted to build one on the common, "near the senter this and the following year."

Captain Samuel Adams, described as a joiner, was chairman of the building committee, and he employed a master carpenter,

* T. W. Higginson, "An American Stonehenge."

Jeremiah Spofford, his wife's brother-in-law, and two others—housewrights from Georgetown, now Bradford, Massachusetts—for the framing. Timothy Palmer, who is credited with the design of the church at Newburyport built twenty-five years later, is also mentioned.

The frame was raised on the 16th or 17th of June—there seems to be some doubt as to the day. There is a story that people, putting their ears to the ground, heard the guns of the British warships in Boston harbor, seventy miles away. The 17th was a Saturday, however, and it is unlikely that the raising, perhaps incomplete at sundown, would have been begun on the last day of the week. Furthermore, another account states that the Georgetown men set out for home the day after, "ride and tie," three men with one horse to carry tools, and at Townsend, in the forenoon, they heard the roar of the guns at Bunker Hill; and coming over the Westford hills in the evening saw the light of Charlestown burning.

Originally the meetinghouse had no tower or steeple. The main entrance was the door seen today in the center of the south side, and there was a porch with entrance at each end. The tower and belfry were built over the west porch in 1823. There are nearly fifteen hundred lights of glass in the windows. Until 1798 the meetinghouse was unpainted.

Like several similar steeples in this region, the elliptical windows and blinds in the upper part are shams, merely painted on the flat boarding. The bell, made in Revere's foundry like so many others, cracked and has been recast. It is still rung for services in the new church. Much curiosity is aroused by the small elliptical window in the tower vestibule, placed so that the sexton could see the minister when he came out of the door of the manse on the other side of the common.

Apparently the interior of the meetinghouse was not finished to the satisfaction of the committee until sometime after the Revolution, for in 1787 it was voted "not to Except" the finishing of the inside; but two years later a committee was appointed to "settle" with Captain Adams. Perhaps the committee was a bit hardboiled, for it was not until 1780, five years after the raising, that an article was put into the warrant "To see if the town will make any allowance to Captain Henry Coffeen for the Barrel of

OLD MEETINGHOUSE (C. 1775) *Jaffrey, New Hampshire*

Rum that he paid for which was expended at the Raising of the meetinghouse." (It was voted that the selectmen settle.)

Originally there were galleries on three sides supported on fluted Doric columns. The pulpit was opposite the center aisle, under the round-arched window on the North side—"built after the English style, high and dignified in appearance," and reached by two flights of steps—with a huge sounding board above. There was a pew in front for the elders and a slip pew for the deacons. The choir was in the gallery over the center entrance, opposite the pulpit. Square pews, about five feet each way, had the "banister" backs of the period and hinged seats on two sides, with room for a chair in the center, usually occupied by an elderly lady of the family. The wall pews were raised one step. Near the pulpit, in front of the "body pews," were free seats for the poor and aged. There was no heating until about 1820, when a stove was set up in the broad aisle in front of the pulpit. Old ladies had foot stoves, filled with coals. At noon the women went to a near-by house to get warm, the men and boys to the tavern, where the men drank flip. Though, as we have seen, the inside of the meetinghouse was not "excepted" until 1789, the pews must have been installed ten years before, for in 1779 it had been voted to sell them to the highest bidder, "except them that have been against paying anything towards building the house."

The panelwork later installed is thought to have been the work of John Buckley, to whom Adams, chairman of the building committee, deeded in 1784 a piece of land on the west side of the road. His charming little white house still stands there, one of the oldest houses in Jaffrey, just below the Shattuck Inn. Buckley, originally Johann Buchler, was a Hessian, probably captured in Burgoyne's army and escaping on the march from Saratoga to Boston in 1777. As Adams had had business dealings with Buckley over the piece of land, what is more likely than that he should arrange to have the German cabinetmaker employed when the interior finish was to be installed in the church? If so, it was perhaps to him that the delay was due when it was voted "not to Except."

After the passage of the Toleration Act in 1819 the four or more different denominations in the town had the use of the meetinghouse in proportion to the value of their property. The arrangement proved unsatisfactory, however. Meanwhile the little manufacturing community of East Jaffrey had been growing up at the falls of the Contoocook River, and in 1831 the Congregationalists built the brick church at the Center. Others built at East Jaffrey, and after 1844 the old meetinghouse was used only for town meetings. It had become dilapidated; the balconies and their supporting columns were torn out, the pulpit and pews destroyed and forgotten. In 1870 the building was remodeled for a town hall, with a room for the high school. Then in 1872 John Conant gave a thousand dollars as the nucleus of a fund for its repair; and in 1926 the Jaffrey Village Improvement Association remodeled the interior to its present condition, with the large stage at the east end.

After the organization of the town in 1773, the extravagant sum of six pounds ("lawful money," worth much more then than now), was voted to support the gospel; with the thrifty provision —mindful that the first man was to have the three hundred acres —that he was to be a *young* man. Apparently there was little competition for the position. The appropriation was finally raised to the extraordinary amount of a thousand pounds (perhaps $130, "lawful money"), for preaching—but "that the s^{d} Com^{ee} do not employ one man more than one sabbath." A number of candidates appeared and disappeared without result. By February, 1781, the town was getting impatient, and voted that "the Com^{ee} for hireing Preaching shall get it as soon as they can." The following month the appropriation was raised again, to twice the second amount—two thousand pounds. Two more candidates had come and gone when at last, in December, 1781, Laban Ainsworth came up for trial; and in July it was voted unanimously to give him a call. The committee reported that he was to have "the North End of the two Sentre Lots, also the mountain Lot, and in money thirty Pounds." Also that the report be given to him "for an incoragement to settle with us in the ministry" and for "a Salary seventy Pounds." The following year it was voted to grant him "liberty annually to visit his Friends twice each year of the two Sabbaths at each time." Evidently Mr. Ainsworth made an immediate impression, and the committee is to be credited with having made a good choice. He served the town for nearly fifty years.

A native of Woodstock, Connecticut, and a graduate of Dartmouth, Ainsworth lived to be over a hundred, remaining as pastor until his death, up to the last year or two of his life without a colleague. He had a withered right arm, on account of which, perhaps, he never wrote his sermons—sometimes, it is said, looking up his text after breakfast Sunday morning.

Across the common from the church, at the corner of the Rindge road looking across the valley towards Little Monadnock and Gap Mountain, stands the fine old house still known as the manse, which Ainsworth built—the second on the site, for his first house was burnt. A young son of Deacon Eleazar Spofford lost his life in the fire. Since the death of Mr. Ainsworth and the building of present church in 1831, the ministers have lived in the house next to it at the corner of Blackberry Lane.

Of the three old inns and hotels that at one time or another have stood around the common, the old red house back of the church, once the Cutter Tavern, is the only one left. John Cutter was landlord, having bought it from his brother Benjamin in 1804. His son John, Jr., in 1808 built the Ark: a big farmhouse on the Dublin road, for more than seventy years famous as a place of entertainment for summer boarders. Some of his descendants continue the family tradition at the Shattuck Inn. The line of the old turnpike was across the common, down the steep road by the burying ground, crossing the present Dublin road and passing the old Buckley house. Traces of the old way are plainly to be seen where it joins the present rough road down the hill, at the lower edge of the common.

In the burying ground beyond the old meetinghouse are the graves of Jaffrey's oldest settlers, Cutters and Pooles and Shattucks, Spauldings and Maynards—names long prominent in the town's history and well known today. Here is a great slate headstone to the memory of Captain Adams, builder of the church, and his wife Lucy. Two old stones leaning side by side in the northeasterly part bear touching epitaphs to two of the town's most deserving, though humble inhabitants.

Fortune came to Jaffrey in 1781. Though he was almost immediately "warned out" in accordance with the practice of the time on the supposition that he would become a public charge, he ignored the order and remained there. He lived about a mile northeast of the old Spofford mills, where he had a small

SACRED
to the memory of
Amos Fortune
who was born free in
Africa, a slave in America
he purchased liberty
professed Christianity
lived respectably, &
died hopefully
Nov. 17, 1801
Aet. 91

SACRED
to the memory of
Violate,
by sale the slave of
Amos Fortune, by marri-
age his wife, by her
fidelity his friend and
solace, she died his widow.
Sept. 13, 1802
Aet. 73.

tannery. Here he prospered to such an extent that on his death in 1801 he was able to leave not only a small legacy to an adopted daughter and provision for gravestones for himself and his wife, but "a handsome present" to the church of which he was a member—"the remaining part, if any there be, to give as a present for the support of the school-house No. 8." The church received a hundred dollars, partly expended for a communion service. To the selectmen was paid $233.95, worth much more then than now. In 1927, the school having been abandoned, it was decided to use the money for prizes in public speaking contests.

Among the numerous widows and wives, maids and spinsters, Betsys, Sallys, and Pollys are much in evidence. In the corner of the ground by the entrance is the old hearse house.

From the westerly slope of the hill on a clear day there is a striking view of the wooded slopes of the mountain, every tree and ledge and rocky precipice standing out in startling relief, from base to summit.

Behind the church, Blackberry Lane leads down the hill to the Thorndike Pond road. Here and along the village street towards East Jaffrey, are many fine old houses and their gardens, belonging to people who have long made Jaffrey their summer home.

There are several other rather notable churches in the Jaffrey region. That at Peterborough is generally believed to have been built from plans by Bulfinch.

Jonathan Smith, a native of Peterborough, used to say that his father had told him that he had "assisted in the purchase" in

FAÇADE OF THE UNITARIAN CHURCH (1825) *Peterborough, New Hampshire*

Boston of a set of plans that had been rejected by another church in Massachusetts; and it is believed by Dr. Weis and others in Lancaster familiar with the history of the church there, that in 1816 the building committee examined the plans later used in Peterborough and decided that the size of the building would be inadequate to their requirement. Apparently Bulfinch sold plans which do not appear in the recorded lists of his work; and this seems to be confirmed by an inspection of the Peterborough church.

The recessed arched panels in the walls, the fan-shaped blind in the gable, the three arched doorways, and other details are all characteristic of Bulfinch's work. On the other hand, the urns at the corners of the tower and some of the other details are crude in execution—just such as a carpenter without the feeling for form and proportion of the earlier craftsmen might be expected to make in attempting, unsupervised, to interpret small-scale working drawings without full-size details. At Lancaster, there is no record of Bulfinch's having visited the church during construction; but we found that Hersey, referred to as the "architect" or "master builder", was an associate or assistant of Bulfinch's. To the critical eye, the difference in the execution and refinement of details is evident.

Searching as usual for an English model—in this case quite likely, as Bulfinch had been in London—Mr. Place suggests Gibbs's spire of St. Mary-le-Strand. The church was built in 1825.

The shallow "chancel" if it may be so called, was remodeled several years ago, when the present pulpit with sounding board was installed, although these "wineglass" pulpits seem to be somewhat out of place in the restoration of buildings of the square meetinghouse type. The slip pews, arranged with center aisle, still have their doors. The organ with black walnut case of the Victorian period, when it was installed, is in the usual place in the gallery over the entrance. Dark red hangings at the back of the platform give color to an interior of considerable interest. The large and well equipped parish house was added to the church in 1926—a memorial to Anne and Mary Morrison and Ruth Morrison Staples.

The grant of land in 1737 including the present town of Peterborough was another of those within the area originally held by the Masonian Proprietors. Though a few pioneers came here in 1739, it was not until ten years later that a permanent settlement was made in the southerly part of the town, by some Scotch Presbyterians, whose early years were spent in constant dread of raids by the Indians, who came from their fishing grounds along the Contoocook River.

The town took its name from the Earl of Peterborough, who had been especially popular for his brilliant campaign in the English expedition against Spain in 1705. Macaulay called him, "if not the greatest, yet assuredly the most extraordinary character of the age."

The Presbyterians established a church here in 1766. John Morrison was their first minister. In course of time the church became Congregational, and finally, following the widespread movement of the time, church and parish became Unitarian.

Brigham Young held a revival in Peterborough, when people came from all the surrounding towns, on horseback and in coaches, to hear him preach. While here he was chosen leader of the Mormon Church on the death of Joseph Smith, and when he left for the West a hundred and thirty-six of the inhabitants are said to have followed him, including the Peterborough girl who became his thirteenth wife. She remained his favorite "for several years."

Largely due to the influence perhaps of those attracted to Peterborough by the MacDowell Colony, the town hall and several other of the newer buildings are notable for their design, so consistent with the general character of an old New England community such as Peterborough. Though in a style of quite a different age and place, the Episcopal church of All Saints, designed by Cram and Ferguson, is notable among the newer churches of America. Flanked by the rectory and parish house, it makes a charming picture against the background of the wooded hillside.

At the little village of Hancock, among the hills at the head of the valley eight miles or so along the Concord road, is another of the group of similar early meetinghouses in this part of southern New Hampshire.

Hancock is another of the towns carved out of the grant to

INTERIOR, UNITARIAN CHURCH (1825) *Peterborough, New Hampshire*

THE VILLAGE STREET *Hancock, New Hampshire*

CHURCH AND TOWN HALL (1820) *Hancock, New Hampshire*

the Masonian Proprietors, from the so-called "Society Land" not already granted for townships. First settlers apparently did not come here until 1764. At the beginning of the Revolution there were only eight or ten families, and some of these stayed for only a short time. The town was incorporated in 1779. John Hancock had come into possession of a large part of "Great Lot" Number 2, and the town was named for him; but he seems never to have taken any especial interest in it, though as late as 1795 his heirs were taxed for nearly two thousand acres.

For the first ten years after settlement town meetings and church services were held in Joseph Symonds's barn. In 1789, following the usual discussions as to site and dimensions of the building, a meetinghouse was raised on the common—a plain "house," with the principal entrance in the middle of the long front and porches at each end, without belfry or steeple.

In 1791 Reed Paige, a graduate of Dartmouth, was ordained, the first settled minister in Hancock. He served his people for a quarter of a century. For six years after his death in 1816 the town was without a settled minister. During the interim, in 1819, the meetinghouse was burnt.

The raising of the frame of the present building the following year required two days, when the ridgepole was "wet down" with a bottle of rum. The building committee had been instructed to follow the design of the church at Dublin, now demolished, which is said to have been a copy of the one at Fitzwilliam. Comparison of the two buildings would seem to verify this, though the Fitzwilliam church has a portico of four Ionic columns instead of the projecting vestibule with pediment, at Hancock, where they thought the portico "unsuitable to a meeting-house." In both spires the elliptical windows of the upper stage are merely painted on the flat surface. Sale of the pews brought seven thousand dollars—sufficient to pay for the building.

Details of cornices, doorways, and spires, similar in both buildings, are elaborate and refined, though both have several examples of a crude "jigsawed" applied ornament which appears to be of later date than the original work. But the exteriors of the Hancock and Fitzwilliam meetinghouses are remarkably fine, and both have been kept well painted and in good repair. Unfortunately so much cannot be said for the interiors.

In 1851 the Hancock church was moved from its original site on the common and "modernized," with the town hall in the lower story—an arrangement which is still continued at Rindge; these being the only two places in New Hampshire where the old union of church and town still prevails.

In 1822 Archibald Burgess had succeeded Paige as the first occupant of the pulpit of the new church, beginning a pastorate of nearly thirty years. He was followed in 1850 by Asahel Bigelow, who served the town for another quarter-century and more, until his death in 1877 at the age of eighty. Thus the pastorates of these three covered a period of nearly ninety years.

It is to be regretted that it has not been possible to restore the interior of the church to something like its original condition. At present the whole is painted a dull drab, with the remains of the crude stencil ornament applied in a hit-or-miss way sometime during the nineteenth century. A flat pressed-steel ceiling covers the auditorium. The pews are placed in a slightly curving arrangement, then considered essential for convenience, without center aisle, and all together the interior is depressing and disappointing after the first promising view of the fine exterior. Inadequate platform furniture is placed at infrequent intervals against the long, flat wall. Worst of all is the great organ in its black walnut case of the period of the other furniture, which occupies the corner of the auditorium at the left of the platform: a long row of chairs in front for the choir, so placed as to stare into the faces of the congregation.

Hancock is a charming, unspoiled village, with an ancient tavern much patronized by summer visitors, and many dignified old white houses. For many years the town has been a resort for people of culture and refinement who have come to spend the summer among the green hills and streams of southern New Hampshire. It is to be hoped that the time may come when it is possible to raise funds for at least a partial restoration of the interior of this fine old meetinghouse, as in the case of the church at Jaffrey, now used as a town and community hall.

The church at Fitzwilliam was the second of several rather notable wooden churches in this region, all built during the first quarter of the nineteenth century, and all nearly identical in design. (It seems to have been a common practice of the time for building committees to be instructed to build a new meetinghouse like one in some neighboring town which happened to meet with the approval of a majority of the congregation. The church at Templeton, Massachusetts, is said to have been the model for the one at Fitzwilliam—copied in turn, as we have seen, at Dublin and Hancock; and there is a similar church at Ashby.) According to the records, Thomas Stratton was paid $3.30 for "assistance" in drawing the plans used for the Fitzwilliam meetinghouse. The building was dedicated late in November of 1816. The following January it was struck by lightning and burnt to the ground. Undaunted, these determined people went to work again; and in a little over a year, early in June, 1818, the frame was raised for another meetinghouse. The ridgepole is said to be a single sixty-foot timber. By Election Day it was finished—a reproduction of the building destroyed.

Proportions and exterior details as at Hancock are remarkably refined, and the cornice and pediment of the portico have the small "triangular" corbel ornaments characteristic of this region. The columns of the portico were turned on the site from solid logs, with their centers bored to prevent checking. The tower and belfry, surmounted by two octagonal stages and a short spire and vane, are identical with those of the church at Hancock. As at Hancock and Jaffrey, the elliptical windows of the upper stage are merely painted on the flat surface. The bell, cast in Paul Revere's foundry, fell to the ground unharmed in the burning of the first meetinghouse, but like so many others it finally had to be recast—cracked by an excited ringer when one of the houses in the town was burning. Three hundred silver dollars contributed by farmers of the town were added to the metal in accordance with the prevailing belief that the silver gave a more musical tone to the bell.

After a view of the beautiful and well cared-for exterior of the building, the shabby interior is disappointing. Originally there were galleries around three sides, with the choir in the rear and seats for negroes in the north end of the west gallery; but the congregation became too small for the old building and in 1857 the little church was built at the south end of the common. In 1868 the upper floor was laid, and the old meetinghouse lost all semblance of the original interior. For many years it has been used as a town hall, and walls and woodwork are now painted a dull drab.

Fitzwilliam was established a century later than most of the towns near the coast, whose settlers came directly from England. Lacking their tender memories of the old country, the people of what thus far had been known as Stoddardtown or Monadnock Number 4, named it on its incorporation in 1773 for Earl Fitzwilliam, a popular person of the time.

Benjamin Bigelow, the first settler in the town, came from Lunenburg, Massachusetts, with his wife about 1761, in an oxcart; and under it, their only shelter until they built a hut, a daughter was born. A monument on the little green in front of the old church claims Brigadier General James Reed as the founder of the town. Reed, who was born in Woburn, Massachusetts, became the proprietor of Lot Number 4 of the Monadnock lands and is said to have built the first house, where for a while he kept an inn. He was an officer in the French and Indian War, colonel in the Second New Hampshire Regiment of Volunteers at Bunker Hill and later a brigadier general in the Continental army.

Fitzwilliam is a pleasant village of fine old white houses and country stores around a little green, with an old tavern once a change house for stages on the turnpike, and now largely patronized by motorists and other summer visitors.

At historic Bennington, among the foothills of the Green mountains of Vermont, the old meetinghouse has one of the finest of all the many cupola-surmounted belfries in New England. Dating from 1805, this was the second church built in the town. During the years it suffered many alterations, and in 1932, on the hundred and fifty-fifth anniversary of the Battle of Bennington, it was proposed to restore the old building to its original condition, the cost being estimated at $30,000. Among the first whose interest and support were sought was President Coolidge; and one of his last acts was to write a letter urging the "thoughtful men and women of the state to lend aid to the plan." With his characteristic moderation he had told Dr. Booth that at that time of financial depression such a thing would be impossible; but nearly $35,000 was contributed, and on August 15, 1937,

THE FIRST CHURCH (1805) *Old Bennington, Vermont*

the hundred and sixtieth anniversary of the battle, the church was rededicated as "Vermont's Colonial Shrine."

The first meetinghouse in Bennington stood on a spot now marked by a monument on the village green. Built in 1763–67, it was the first Protestant church in the New Hampshire Grants. The legislature met there eight different times, and stirring scenes took place within its walls. Although it stood for nearly forty years, it probably was never entirely finished; travelers through the town described it as "a dilapidated structure." Before the end of the eighteenth century a new building was badly needed, but it was not until 1805 that the present church was built—one of the number supposed to have been inspired by that much-used book of Asher Benjamin's, "The Country Builder's Assistant," first published in 1797. Lavius Fillmore, born in Norwich, Connecticut, is known to have been the architect, though his name does not appear in the Bennington records. The next year he was called upon to build the larger church at Middlebury, apparently as a result of his success at Bennington. He was a second cousin of President Millard Fillmore.

The church was first altered in 1840, when the original high pulpit and box pews were removed; and on three other occasions further alterations were made. The most deplorable devastation occurred after the Civil War, in 1865. From accounts we have, one would think that, after that, little could have remained of the original interior but the six Ionic columns, each turned from a single white pine. But, in the restoration, the "apse" with its massive walnut pulpit was removed, and the high Asher Benjamin pulpit with the Palladian window over it reconstructed. The forty-eight box pews on the floor and those in the side and rear galleries were rebuilt—those in the galleries largely with parts of the old ones which had been used for the long pews installed in their place.

For several decades the unmarried men were seated in the north gallery; the maids and spinsters, in the south. Perhaps the trousered young women of today carry jackknives; but while those old pew backs on their side of the house remain unscarred as when they were built, those on the opposite side are liberally carved with the initials of their one-time young occupants, with various attempts apparently intended for portraiture, both animal and human, and even references to Scripture texts. The two long and narrow box pews over the stairwells were for negro servants. The paneling of these was nearly seven feet high—an arrangement by which the occupants, while recognizing that "a place for them too" was provided, might not offend the sensibilities of their benefactors by being seen.

Old Bennington is on a hill above the newer commercial center of the town. In 1749 Governor Benning Wentworth granted this township west of the Connecticut River, and it was named for him. According to Mr. Van de Water, the Governor had an abiding faith in "Bual Madeira, old rum, fair women, good food, brilliant raiment, money, influence," and above all, Benning Wentworth. He liked pomp and circumstance; and the progress of his four-horse coach with red-coated postilions through the streets of Portsmouth was a spectacle not to be missed. Wentworth may have believed that he had sufficient reason to consider that the area west of the Connecticut came within the bounds of the New Hampshire Grants. The King's charter had described Connecticut's western boundary as the Pacific Ocean and that of Massachusetts the same. New Hampshire's western boundary was more vague. It extended "till it meets our other governments." New York's charter bestowed by Charles II in 1664 upon his brother, the Duke of York, gave that province's eastern boundary as the Connecticut River, and New York naturally disputed New Hampshire's claim. So that the Bennington grant was the beginning of a long and hard-fought controversy which at one time threatened to end in actual warfare and bloodshed between the contending parties.

The first settlement within the disputed area had been made by Captain Samuel Robinson, who came from Hardwick, Massachusetts, in 1761 with half a dozen families. Bennington was the center of hostilities, and this was the region of most of the skirmishing between the "Bennington Mob" and Sheriff Ten Eyck with several hundred armed men sent into Vermont by the governor of New York. The meeting place of the Vermonters was Captain Stephen Fay's Catamount Tavern. When at length Governor Tryon and his council decided to adopt more conciliatory measures, it was in the old meetinghouse that the people assembled to hear their communication.

FAÇADE OF THE FIRST CHURCH *Old Bennington, Vermont*

ST. MICHAEL'S CHURCH (1714) *Marblehead, Massachusetts*

But the chief interest of historic Bennington of course centers about the battle, although actually it was not fought in Bennington or even in Vermont, but six miles away in the Walloomsac valley, over in New York State. Once more the Committee of Safety was meeting at the Catamount Tavern, where with Ethan Allen they had met in 1775 to plan the capture of Ticonderoga. In the summer of 1777 Burgoyne had recaptured the fort and was marching down the Champlain valley with his hired German regiments and some Indians, apparently bent upon the capture of horses and much-needed supplies known to be stored at Bennington. Colonel John Stark was put in command of the Vermont troops and those sent to his assistance from New Hampshire. Stark had fought in the French War and at Bunker Hill and Trenton and other battles of the Revolution. Disgusted when Congress promoted Benjamin Lincoln and other less deserving officers of lower rank, he had returned to his farm in New Hampshire. On the 13th of August, Baum was approaching with his entire force of Brunswickers, Hessians, and a party of Indians, some fourteen hundred strong. Stark, who had been organizing his forces at Charlestown, on the other side of the Connecticut, had sent a small detachment on to Manchester, in advance. They came through the pass between the hills in the present town of Peru. There is a high point along the road today where we pause to take in that wide sweep over the valley below: its green fields and woodlands and distant upland pastures, and the long ridge of Stratton Mountain showing endwise in the south.

On the night of the 14th rain began to fall, becoming a heavy downpour. Parson Allen of Pittsfield, who had come with militia from Berkshire, complained to Stark that the Berkshire people had been called out several times "to no purpose," and would not go out again if they were not allowed to fight now. Asked if he would have them fall to in the rain and dark, the parson admitted that just then the conditions were unsatisfactory. "As soon as the Lord sends us sunshine," said Stark, "if I do not give you fighting enough, I'll never ask you to come out again." Next morning, the 16th, the sun rose on a hot summer day, with clouds of mist rising from the Walloomsac River, above fields of ripening corn and wheat. "Those redcoats are ours today, or Molly Stark's a widow!" And they were. (Though Stark's wife's name was Elizabeth, history has had it otherwise.) The Indians fled in panic, for "the woods were full of Yankees." Parson Allen, mounting a stump, exhorted the enemy to lay down their arms; then coming down from his perch, exchanged his Bible for a gun.

Through all of that hot August day and until after sundown, the fight continued. Two hundred of the enemy were dead and six hundred prisoners were marched to Bennington, many of them to be lodged in Parson Dewey's old meetinghouse. Some of the dead lie in the old burying ground beside the church. The American loss was thirty killed and forty wounded. A thousand stands of arms and four fieldpieces were captured, and Washington considered the battle to be decisive of the fate of Burgoyne, who sent a gloomy account to England of his situation following the disaster.

The battle monument stands on the summit of the hill where once stood the stone storehouse the Brunswickers and Hessians were sent to capture. A high tapering shaft of Vermont granite, in the form of an obelisk, it rises more than three hundred feet above the hilltop, overlooking the Vermont landscape of green valleys and forest-clad mountains, reaching away ridge beyond ridge towards the far horizon: to the west, from whence came those meddlesome "Yorkers" against the Bennington "mob;" to the south, Greylock and the other green Berkshire Hills of Parson Allen's Berkshire militia.

There are two other fine churches which should be seen in the beautiful western foothills of the Green Mountain range near Lake Champlain. We found that Lavius Fillmore built a larger church at Middlebury the year after he finished that at Bennington. Though he has been said to have "reproduced" the Bennington church, there are marked differences between the two. In place of the cupola, Middlebury has a tall spire, "closely resembling the steeple of St. Martin's-in-the-Fields, Trafalgar Square, in London." Somewhat resembling it, would be nearer the truth, though it is a fine wooden spire. Interiors of both buildings have a plaster dome ceiling, but Middlebury originally had the unique plan of the pulpit in the center surrounded by circular pews.

At Burlington is a brick church of remarkably fine design;

and certain features of the exterior suggest that it is correctly attributed to Peter Banner, architect of the Park Street Church in Boston. The motif of the entrance door with the window above it, the proportions of the wooden steeple with rather high arched belfry, the many-lighted, round-topped windows in the second octagon, and the tapering spire and vane—all are charming.

X

ALONG THE NORTHERN SHORE: ST. MICHAEL'S, MARBLEHEAD, AND THE FIRST CONGREGATIONAL CHURCH AT NEWBURYPORT

HISTORICALLY, one of the most important of all the early New England churches is old St. Michael's, Marblehead. Built in 1714, nine years before Christ Church, Boston, it is the fourth oldest Episcopal church in New England, only those of Boston, Newbury, and Newport being older. It is also the second oldest Episcopal church building still standing, preceded only by St. Paul's, North Kingston, Rhode Island, now removed to Wickford, which was built in 1707.

Marblehead, which was set off from Salem in 1649, became a principal port for fishing vessels along the New England coast, and had a large and profitable foreign trade, especially with Bilbao, Spain.

By 1707 subscriptions amounting to over £400 had been made, and in 1714 nearly £400 more was subscribed by members of King's Chapel, "in Order to the Building and Erecting a Handsome Church in the Town of Marblehead." Of the thirty-four names preserved in the church records as benefactors, twenty-nine were sea captains. Colonel Francis Nicholson, ever zealous for the English Church in the colonies, headed the list, and he was asked to name the church. In 1714, the rector of King's Chapel went to England and arranged with the Society for the Propagation of the Gospel to send missionaries to Marblehead and Newbury, and in that same year the church was built. In none of the accounts is anything said of architect or builder.

William Shaw, an Oxonian, was the first rector. When about this time the Congregationalists built a second church in town,

Shaw wrote home that they had built it "in Damnable Spite and Malice against our church, as some of their chief members have openly declared," and Judge Sewall noted: "This morning Bows, a young man, tells me he is fin'd 20s for saying that the new Church of England minister of Marblehead inveigh'd in his Sermon against Extempore Prayers, affirm'd the Dissenters in doing it broach'd damnable Blasphemies."

During Shaw's occasional absences, the rector of King's Chapel, Samuel Myles, sometimes took the services at St. Michael's; and from the beginning the church was a favored foster child of the Chapel.

Queen Anne, ever a friend of the Episcopal Church in the colonies, had died in the year of the building of St. Michael's, to be succeeded by "the heavy, vulgar German prince who represented the Protestant cause of liberty." The members of the church at Marblehead signed the "humble address" prepared by the ministers and others of King's Chapel, to the "High and Mighty Prince George Elector of Brunswick-Lunenburg," whom they "humbly approach . . . with the most sincere and hearty Joy for your peaceful accession to the Crown,—yours by superior Right and Merit,—A Blessing so great as mitigates our sorrows for the demise of your Royal predecessor of happy Memory, who was always to Us a Gratious and Bountiful Sovereign."

Following which, it is interesting to note that the second rector was David Mossom, who removed after nine years to St. Peter's Church, New Kent County, Virginia, where he performed the marriage ceremony for George Washington and Mrs. Custis. Let us hope he fared better there, for of St. Michael's he wrote: "Our Church is plain but neat. . . . I receive nothing from the people but the contributions collected after Divine service on the Lord's days at the Church, most of which depends upon Strangers; taken one with another they are computed between 20 and 30 Shillings this money, which is the most extended value and does not amount to 10 Shillings Sterling. I have neither house nor Glebe, but am obliged to hire a house myself, for which I pay out of my own pocket £25 per ann., the Parish contributing nothing towards it." This is confirmed by the Fulham Palace records of the Bishop of London: "Marblehead,—There is no house nor glebe; the voluntary contributions very precarious." Very different, certainly, from the fat livings and comfortable rectories of England.

Cutler, of Christ Church, disliked Mossom, and wrote maliciously at the time of his leaving, to his friend Dr. Zachary Gray, "A good-for-nothing Clergyman . . . is now, I hope, taking his final leave of us." Mossom had performed good and faithful service at Marblehead, however. He said to John Barnard of the First Church: "Why, sir, before I came over to you, I was filled with the conception of you as an heathenish, irreligious people, full of spleen and rancour against the Church of England; but when I had been among you some time, I found you a virtuous, religious, civilized people, and of moderate temper towards the Church; and therefore I thought proper to alter my conduct."

There was constant opposition from the Congregationalists over the observance of Christmas Day and other church festivals. In reply to a sermon by Barnard, Mossom's successor, George Pigot, said: "I *wish* . . . that the vile Rout and Firing of Guns, at *Marblehead* on *Christmas-Day* were suppressed by *Authority;* and that the same Respect at least were paid to *that* Day, and the *Thirtieth* of *January,* from his People, as is given by Church-Men to their *Thanksgiving* and *Fast* Days."

Pigot, who had been educated in England, was a claimant to the baronies of Morley and Monteagle and wished to go to assert his claim. The church authorities apparently objected, however, for it was not until six years later, when ill health compelled him to resign, that he finally returned to England. In the winter of 1736, after a visit to a poor and sick parishioner, he had fallen on the ice and broken an arm. In England he obtained the rectory of Chaldon in Surrey, but lived only about a year. It is thought that his wife never left Marblehead, for she was buried there behind the church fifteen years later.

During Mr. Pigot's rectorate the church was enlarged, and the next forty years were a period of prosperity. Joshua Wingate Weeks, rector at the outbreak of the Revolution, wrote to the secretary of the Society for the Propagation of the Gospel that most of the young people of any note in the town attended it, and "that Marblehead has elected the only churchman who sits in the General Assembly."

But when the British Parliament passed the Stamp Act

THE ALTAR OF ST. MICHAEL'S CHURCH (1714) *Marblehead, Massachusetts*

zealous Marbleheaders missed no opportunity to denounce the Church of England. And as though the people of St. Michael's had not trouble enough on their hands the enthusiast Whitefield chose the time to pay a visit to Marblehead, where he "fiercely attacked in 'the most abusive language the church, the rector, and all belonging to it.' "

At the beginning of the Revolution Marblehead had become the second town of the colony in population and in wealth, with forty ships engaged in foreign trade, and a great number of the people wanted a Church of England service. But all this was changed with the outbreak of the Revolution. On the passing of the Boston Port Bill by the British Parliament, forbidding ships to enter or leave the port of Boston until the East India Company had been indemnified for its tea, the seat of government was moved to Salem; Marblehead was made a port of entry, and its wharves and warehouses were placed at the disposal of the Boston merchants. But it was a divided parish. The rector avowed himself a Loyalist, and when, after the signing of the Declaration of Independence, the law was passed by the Provincial Congress forbidding the use of the liturgy, the church was closed. On the news of the Declaration, a mob had broken into the building, pulled down the royal arms, and rung the bell until it cracked. For a while services were held in private houses, until the rector was obliged to seek refuge in Nova Scotia.

The church was opened again on the 6th of February, 1780, when Woodward Abraham, the seventh rector, read prayers and a sermon. He conducted the services for six years. Oddly enough, it was Samuel Sewall, Chief Justice of the Supreme Court of Massachusetts and a descendant of the old Puritan, who led the movement to have the church reopened.

For many years now the history of the parish was one of sad struggles and sorrowful experiences. In 1813 John Prentiss Kewley Henshaw (later, Bishop of Rhode Island) was rector, at a salary of $500; and after five years he was succeeded, with a stipend of only $400 and the proceeds of a glebe, by Benjamin Bosworth Smith, who became presiding bishop of the Episcopal Church in the United States. For some years the church was closed and deserted. The glebe and rectory became hopelessly involved and were sold to pay parish debts. About this time the Unitarian movement in New England was at its height, and in 1821 some of the local seceding Congregationalists were looking for a church. One of the more influential of these was William Reed, who looked with covetous eyes upon old St. Michael's. He bought pews, and actually became a proprietor and vestryman. Finally he induced a number of other proprietors to petition the legislature to repeal the old charter granted in 1799 and reincorporate it as a "Congregational Meeting-house." But this attempt to do away with the old church put new life into the parish, and some of the proprietors, led by Dr. Drury, an old and influential vestryman, and Captain Trevett, an old sea captain, obtained the support of the bishop and the rector of the church at Salem and succeeded in persuading the legislature to deny the petition. For a few years services were resumed, only to be given up again, and for four years the church once more remained closed.

It was in 1833, during the one-year rectorate of George Eastman, that the old square pews were torn out and the chancel changed to the north.

In 1872 there came one of the most influential rectors in St. Michael's history—John Wickliffe Leek. His short rectorate is noteworthy for the great improvements made in the building's surroundings. When he came, it could only be reached by a twelve-foot alleyway from Washington Street, past the back yards of some old houses. One old tenement house, with yard and outhouses directly in front of the church door, almost entirely hid it from the street. Mr. Leek at once went to work to secure the removal of the house. The requisite amount for its purchase was raised, and in the summer of 1874 it was removed, a ledge of rocks blasted away, the area graded and seeded, and a driveway laid out. During this same year, the daughters of Mrs. Eunice Hooper bought the property adjoining and built a rectory as a memorial to their mother.

During the rectorate of Mr. Leek's successor, Julius H. Ward, the church had a narrow escape from destruction in Marblehead's great fire of the 25th of June, 1877. The roof caught fire and the historic old building seemed doomed; but a young man, Thomas Gorman, managed to get upon the roof, and while the rector held him by a rope from the belfry, he put the fire out.

The rather homely little church stands on Summer Street, once Frog Lane, and is one of the few Church of England buildings distinctly of the meetinghouse plan. Originally there were seven gables, which probably leaked badly, for about 1728 they were covered with the present plain hipped roof. A squat, square tower rises awkwardly from the roof at the front. In a letter to Colonel Nicholson, to whom the establishment of St. Michael's Church at Marblehead was primarily due, the committee wrote that they had "erected and raised" a church with a tower "50 foot from the Ground and 17 foot square, and we design the spire 53 foot above the Tower. . . . We have agreed for finishing the whole, having all things in place. But the weather proving extreme hard has put us by for the present, but hope by the blessing of God to compleat and finish the whole by the last of June ensuing at the farthest." But the tower was never built. If it had been, and the dimensions as given were correct, perhaps the little church might in truth have seemed to its builders "a beautiful little edifice," though today it is rather hard to imagine it. If, as we are told, all of the material was brought from England, it must have been that no suitable timber was to be found on the rock-bound coast adjacent to Marblehead.

The arrangement of the interior has been altered several times. Originally there were two doors, that at the west having been removed in 1771. There is a tradition that a door was cut in the west side of the church to accommodate a stout gentleman who was too large to get through an ordinary pew door; a story seemingly substantiated by a recorded vote of the parish: "That at present it is convenient to keep open the door leading into the garden belonging to the estate of the late William Bourne, Esq."

In 1728 ten or fifteen feet was added to the north side, when the pulpit was moved back, thus placing it on the long axis; but the chancel remained on the east side until 1833. At that time the old square pews were taken out and the chancel changed to the north, changing the interior to a "church" plan. Only the south gallery, with the organ, remains now. The organ, first mentioned sometime before 1762, came from old St. Paul's in New York. Originally it had been placed in a gallery built for it on the west side. The high "wineglass" pulpit with sounding board, remodeled and rather spoiled in 1833, remained for another ninety years or more.

The reredos with its Decalogue in ancient lettering is the one brought from England when the church was built. The royal crown and arms of George I gave place to a handsome gilded eagle, for some unknown reason in turn removed and replaced by a gilt cross painted on the wall. The present altar and rail were installed in 1937. The crucifix now above the reredos was the gift of the commander of the 101st Infantry in the First World War, in memory of Lieutenant Lyman Rollins, rector of the church and chaplain with the Yankee Division in France. Lieutenant (or Mr.) Rollins received the Croix de Guerre at St. Mihiel.

The church is still lighted by candles in the fine old brass chandelier, gift, in 1732, of John Elbridge, the Collector of the Port of Bristol, England.

In the tower is the bell once recast by Paul Revere. Except for a short time during the Revolution, it has rung out over the old town for more than two hundred and thirty years. Under the church and in the little burying ground behind it are the graves of former clergy and parishioners. Peter Bours, the fifth rector (1753–63), lies here. He was only thirty-six when he died. His portrait by Blackburn, painted as a gift to the church, hangs in the Widener Library at Harvard. To pay for it he sold his black boy, Pompey.

Today Marblehead is among the historic towns of New England to which visiting tourists flock in summer; and before the war, in the racing season, its snug little landlocked harbor between the mainland and the "Neck" was crowded with pleasure craft of every description. Its steep and narrow and crooked streets ("You see," said an old Marbleheader, "they built the houses fust, and the streets afterwards"), with their dignified and historic mansions and many weather-worn and picturesque smaller ones, still look much as they did fifty or a hundred years ago. It is not difficult to people them again with the King's officers and their press gangs that roamed the town in search of crews for His Majesty's ships. The snug harbor was a haven for smugglers, and on dark nights, while the discreet among the population kept well within doors, wisely oblivious to the tramp of feet and rattle of stones on the steep ways up from the beach, many a valuable cargo—ultimate destination, Boston—was safely landed. Almost in the shadow of St. Michael's, the pirate Quelch sought refuge, and Major Sewall chased him nearly to the Isles of Shoals. Blackler, who commanded at the ferry that took Washington across the Delaware for the victory at Trenton, once sat in one of St. Michael's old square pews. The town has always been a haven for seafaring and sea-loving people, and though it long ago ceased to be a shipping port, in normal times many a trim pleasure craft is built and launched from its shipyards.

On leaving Marblehead, we may take a passing glance at the South Church in near-by Salem. Built in 1804 and attributed to Samuel McIntire, this is nearly a counterpart of one which we shall see at Newburyport.

For extreme refinement and elegance of ornamental detail, both exterior and interior, the meetinghouse of the First Church in Newburyport is surpassed by only a few old New England churches. It stands on Pleasant Street in the center of the town, rather crowded by shops and business buildings which have grown up all about it.

Whether this church is actually the work of Samuel McIntire seems to be a matter of doubt. The church at Newburyport and the South Church at Salem are almost exactly alike with the exception of some minor details. That at Newburyport was built first, in 1801, and Timothy Palmer (some say Andrews Palmer), a builder, is recorded as the architect, though there is a tradition that McIntire designed it. If he did not, he would seem to have copied it for his Salem church, built three years later, and the praise bestowed upon him for Salem is due to someone else. Timothy Palmer, a native of Boxford, had directed the building of the Merrimac bridge in 1792. More than a thousand feet long, it was a creditable feat of engineering for a country architect and builder. The year before he built the Newburyport church he had been made "surveyor of the highways," and under his skilful supervision the roads and lanes of the town were greatly improved.

All the proportions and details of the three entrance doorways and other parts of the façade are remarkably perfect in design and workmanship, and the slender spire and octagonal lantern with delicate engaged columns above the arched belfry are particularly fine in the elegance of their scale and proportions.

The interior is notable for the elaboration and fine workmanship of its delicately scaled ornament, particularly on the gallery fronts. The high pulpit on slender fluted columns is unusually well proportioned, though the staircases probably were later additions, when the entrance at the back was closed. The architectural motif with its crimson draperies is especially happy, supplying the all-important interest so commonly lacking on the blank walls facing the congregations of many old meetinghouses.

"Newbury was planted in 1634. My father has told me so, who was one of the *first* inhabitants." So wrote Judge Sewall in his diary, and he ought to have known. Sewall probably wrote the inscription on his father's gravestone in the old burying ground of the first parish in Newbury: "Henry Sewall, sent by his father, Henry Sewall in the ship Elizabeth and Dorcas, arrived at Boston 1634, *wintered* at Ipswich, *helped begin* this plantation 1635 . . ." Coffin, in his "History of Newbury," accounts for the difference in dates by the fact that up to 1752, when the change was made by act of Parliament, the calendar year began on the fifteenth of March. Though the time of settlement has been given as early as 1633, evidence seems to be in favor of the later date.

In 1634 twenty-two ships arrived in New England. In one of these came Thomas Parker and about a hundred others who "went to sit down" at Agawam (Ipswich); "but he choosing rather to accompany some of his countrymen (who came out of Wiltshire in England), to that new place . . . at Newbury." It is said that they came by water from Ipswich through Plum Island Sound and up the stream now called Parker River, after their minister, landing on the north bank a little less than half a mile below the bridge. With them were Henry Sewall and forty or fifty others, and more soon followed. According to tradition Parker preached his first sermon under a large oak which stood on the bank of the river about a hundred yards below the bridge.

A meetinghouse was soon built (1635) on the "lower green" at Newbury Old Town, with the first burying ground near it. In a few years, "weighing the streights they were in" for the want of land suitable for cultivation, distance from the common, "scarcity of fencing stuffe and the like," they decided to move

FAÇADE DETAIL, CHURCH OF THE FIRST RELIGIOUS SOCIETY *Newburyport*

THE SPIRE, CHURCH OF THE FIRST RELIGIOUS SOCIETY (1801) *Newburyport*

from this first settlement on the banks of the river to the "new town." As usual there was "contention" over the location of the meetinghouse, and a long and wordy petition was sent to the General Court by those who were opposed to "removing." Finally the building was placed upon a "knowle of upland"—the northwest corner of the burying ground of the First Parish.

The many real hardships which all these early settlers had to contend with make it hard to understand their constant bickerings over matters which seem to us so trivial and even ludicrous. With the building of each new meetinghouse there arose the inevitable controversy over the seating. "In consequence of 'divers complaints having been made from time to time of disorder in the meeting-house,' and believing that 'the abuses in the youth cannot be so easily reformed, unless every house-holder knows his seat in the 'meeting house,' the selectmen, the twenty-fourth of January, 1651, 'herby order that every house-holder both men and women shall sit in those seats, that are appointed for them during their lives, and not to presse into those seats where they are full already, . . . and the young men are appointed to sit in the four backer seats in the gallery and in the two lower seats at the west door.'" Whereby no doubt some of the disorder was "reformed."

When, about 1660, a new meetinghouse was built on a site near the one then in use, it had a gallery "at both ends and all along on the west side . . . with three payre of stayres," and Henry Jaques who built it was to provide "all the stuff both planks, boards, rayles, and juyces and nayles," for which he was to have "thirty pounds in good current pay or provisions" besides all the "old stuffe of the old gallery in the old meeting house." Apparently much of the work was done in separate contracts, for Jaques was also to lay a "floore all over the meeting house," the town to provide the "juyces" and other materials. When this new house was "seated" the men and women were assigned to separate seats. The galleries were considered the most desirable parts of the house. In the "foreseat" of the west gallery, were thirteen men, "which are as many as can comfortably set in it."

There seems to have been no ordinary in Newbury until 1670, when Hugh March opened a tavern "near the head of Marlborough Street on the spot where [in 1845] John and Stephen Ilsley lived." March had not been in business long, however, before he entered a complaint that Captain Paul White, who had been licensed to "sell wine out of dores by retaile for the necessary relief to some sick or other indigent persons" and to "accomodate the churches occasions," had sold to the inhabitants and others to the "damage and disabling" of the petitioner. The quantity of wine used upon sacramental occasions no doubt was generous.

With Parker in that small band of 1635 had come James Noyes, a young clergyman of twenty-seven. Parker, whose nephew he was, refers to him as "my worthy colleague," and together they served the community for more than twenty years, when Noyes died. Parker lived to be eighty-two, dying in 1677. He was a son of Robert Parker—whom Cotton Mather described as "one of the greatest scholars in the English nation"—and had been at Oxford and later in Dublin and Holland. At Newbury, in addition to his duties as minister, he kept a school, but "took no pay for his pains, unless any present were freely sent him." We are not told what he taught, but a hundred and fifty years later the town voted "not to have arithmetic in the two extremes of the town, but in the centre grammar school only." Another of Parker's nephews, the Reverend Nicholas Noyes wrote: "Though he was blind, yet such was his memory, that he could in his old age teach *Latin, Greek* and *Hebrew,* very artificially." Dr. Popkin, who had the church a century and a half later, tells the story that some ministers, being dissatisfied with some of Parker's opinions, came to reason with him on those subjects. When "they addressed him in English, he replied in Latin; they followed him in Latin, he retired to Greek, and to Hebrew; they pursued; but in Arabic he stopped them."

Of Parker and Noyes, Mather says: "They taught in one school [in England], came over in *one ship;* were pastor and teacher in *one church;* and Mr. Parker continuing always in celibacy, they lived in *one house,* till death separated them for a time." Noyes was of "so loving, and compassionate, and humble carriage, that there were none but desired the continuance of his society."

John Woodbridge also had come with the first small group in 1635. He was ordained in 1644 and went back to England in 1647, returning to Newbury in 1663, when he was engaged "to assist his uncle Parker," when, "for his encouragement" the town voted him thirty pounds for the first half-year. For a while he preached at a salary of sixty pounds a year. For more than twenty years the town had been "agitated" over church government and discipline. As usual, this was finally taken to the courts, where it continued, a long drawn-out controversy, for another ten years. Partly as a result of this, apparently, though both Parker and Woodbridge were "highly esteemed," the town "agreed to employ" Woodbridge no longer.

Towards the end of Parker's pastorate the meetinghouse was again "seated," when the selectmen "granted liberty" to five persons to build a pew for their wives "at the east end of the south gallery to the pulpit," said to be the first pew built in the meetinghouse. This same year the town ordered that no horses should be "tyed *outside* the meeting house fence." At the next meeting, several horses were found tied *inside* the fence. Whereupon it was ordered that "no horses shall be tyed *within* side or *without* side the fence."

Not long before this there had occurred a curious episode which throws a sidelight upon the state of mind which later could produce the fanatical ravings of the witchcraft delusion. In May of 1663 Lydia Wardwell, wife of Eliakim Wardwell of Hampton, walked into the Newbury meetinghouse stark naked, in the midst of service; "seeing the wickedness of your priests and rulers . . . who were . . . blinded with ignorance and persecution, . . . as a sign to them she went in naked amongst them (though it was exceeding hard to her modest and shamefaced disposition,) which put them into such a rage, instead of consideration, they soon laid hands on her, and to the next court at Ipswich had her, where without law they condemned her to be tyed to the fence-post of the tavern where they sat—and there sorely lashed her with twenty or thirty cruel stripes."

Church records of 1664 state "that about this time began the blasting of the wheat to be perceived." This was believed by the Quakers and others to be a judgment from God against the people of Massachusetts for their cruel persecutions. Such opinions were held at this time by all denominations. If any calamity fell upon their opponents, it was a judgment. If on themselves, it was a trial.

In December of 1698 the "old" town of Newbury voted that Sergeant Jaques "should build a meeting-house sixty feet in length fifty feet in breadth and twenty feet in the stud for five hundred and thirty pounds"; in the following February, that it should be "twenty-five feet post instead of twenty," and that the builder should have "twenty pounds more." Strangely there appears seldom to have been any dispute over these absurdly brief and inadequate agreements and specifications, though their authors could quarrel for years over matters which seem to us of little importance.

This meetinghouse, built in 1700, the fourth in Old Newbury, stood until 1806. According to an old wood cut it was plain and square, something like the "Old Ship" at Hingham, with a hipped roof topped by the "turret" in which the bell was hung. Originally it had a "dormar" window on each side, but both windows were for some reason removed. The children sat on seats in the alley, fixed to the outside of the pews. Before the pulpit and the deacons' seat, was a large pew containing a table, where sat the chiefs of the fathers. The turret was in the center, and the bell was rung and tolled in the middle of the broad aisle. Originally, the space was open to the roof, where were "many ornaments of an antique sculpture and wainscot, and it was, in the day of it, a stately building, but long before it was torn down, a steeple was substituted for the turret." One would like to know just what the "many ornaments of an antique sculpture" were, in a meetinghouse raised by people who so hated all ornaments in their religion.

Captain Samuel Sewall was instructed "to procure a good and sufficient meeting house bell for the towne of Newbury, suitable for our towne considering the remoteness of our dwellings." This was a matter that could not be so easily settled, however, and later Sergeant Jaques was "ordered" to hang the old bell in the new "turret." But finally "colonel Daniel Pierce esquire, and Tristram Coffin esquire were impowered to procure a bell of about four hundred pounds weight." Evidently the Colonel was in favor just then, for it was voted at the same time that he should have "first choice for a pew." The minister's wife was to have a pew built for her "by the pulpit stairs," well under the eye of her lord and master. In general the seats were to be arranged like those in the old building, "except ten feet on each side for pews and alleys."

In 1806 this building was moved a little distance from the new one and fitted up for a courthouse, town house, and school, and on the 4th of May John S. Popkin "preached for the last time in the old meeting-house in the first parish, Newbury. It was torn down May sixth." On the 16th of June there was a total eclipse of the sun, and the sills of the new meetinghouse, the fifth in Old Newbury, were laid. On the 17th of September the new house was dedicated.

The first meetinghouse in the part of the town afterwards set apart as Newburyport was built in 1725. On the 17th of February of that year William Moody of Byfield wrote to Judge Sewall: "Our people at towne are going to build another meeting house, but intend to set it so nigh to Mr. Toppan's, that I fear it will make great contention. Newbury are great sufferers this day for what have happened by contending about the place of a meeting house." Writing of this building a hundred years ago, Coffin said: "On this day, the . . . meeting-house, now the first in Newburyport, was dedicated. The sermon was preached by the reverend John Tufts of Newbury. The house was at first forty-five by sixty feet, in length and breadth, but, in 1736, was enlarged, thus making it sixty by eighty feet. It stood in what is now the market place, in Newburyport, the steeple fronting the river. The pulpit, which was on the westerly side, standing near where the town pump now stands."

Meetinghouses were built in West Newbury and Byfield when they were set off as separate parishes, and a study of Coffin's History leaves one with the impression that, if the early settlers were constantly involved in religious controversies, those of Newbury at least had the courage of their convictions; for they seem to have been constantly building new churches. That in Federal Street was raised in 1756, "one hundred feet long and sixty broad, and not one oath was heard and nobody hurt."

Newburyport church and other records of the seventeenth and eighteenth centuries include references to an almost incredible number of earthquakes. One is almost inclined to believe that these people, so prone to obsessions and mental distortions of all kinds, were sometimes victims of their own imaginations. These occurrences were continually noted by Matthias Plant, the Church of England rector.

In 1742 he wrote: "March 27th, a quarter before 7 A.M. the noise of the earthquake was very loud, but it did not make any shaking, as I could perceive. . . . One thing I took notice of namely, at all times before, when we heard the noise, which way our faces were, that way the noise always seemed to be, but now the noise seemed to be behind me, and my family took notice of it that the noise seemed to be behind them." Again; "August 10th [1743], about five P.M. a pretty loud shock of the earthquake." And again on August 2, 1746: "Just before sunrise, there was a considerable loud and long earthquake."

Note that in the last two cases he merely says they were "loud," while in the first he distinctly states that he could not "perceive" any shaking. In other accounts the occurrences seem to have been very definitely earthquakes, however. Coffin quotes four lengthy descriptions of one on the 29th of October, 1727. Of this Matthias Plant wrote: "It continued very terrible by frequently bursting and shocking our houses and lasted all that week . . ."

Another said: "It came with a dreadful roreing, as if it was thunder, and then a pouncer like grate guns. . . . It lasted about two minits. . . . The first night it broke out in more than ten places in ye town in ye clay low land, blowing up ye sands, sum more, sum less. In one place, near Spring island it blew out, as it was judged twenty loads, and when it was cast on coals in ye night, it burnt like brimstone."

Henry Sewall wrote to his kinsman, the Judge: "From sixteen to twenty loads of fine sand thrown out where the ground broke, and several days after the water boiled out like a spring."

Plainly, this was a season of "trials," for in September of that year Stephen Jaques says: "On Saturday in ye afternoon ye wind began to be very strong and increased more in the night. It blew down and brake six trees in my ould orchard and trees all over ye woods. . . . It raised a great tide, which swept away near two hundred load of hay, that was in a swath."

Both Newbury and Portsmouth took a prominent part in the French War. In November of the first year Captain Donahue sailed in a small privateer with sixty men and captured two

French vessels loaded with supplies. On the 2nd of February, 1745, the Reverend Thomas Smith of Portland wrote in his journal: "Great talk about Whitefield's preaching and the fleet to Cape Breton." It is a question which caused more excitement: the religious controversies or the expedition to Louisburg.

One might think that by this time the "chief fathers" would have ceased to concern themselves over the personal idiosyncrasies of their neighbors; but in May of 1752 the members of the church in West Newbury met "to deal with our brother Richard Bartlett. . . . First, our said brother refuses communion with the church for no other reason but because the pastor wears a wigg, and because the church justifies him in it . . . and he sticks not from time to time to assert with the greatest assurance that all who wear wiggs, unless they repent of that particular sin before they die will certainly be damned, which we judge to be a piece of uncharitable and sinful rashness." All this to-do about their headgear in a town, which, according to a census of the time, had fifty slaves—negroes and Indians. "Periwigs" had been an obsession with Judge Sewall, who had them constantly on his mind if not on his head. There are numerous references to them in his diary:

"1685, September 15th. Three admitted to the church, two wore periwigs."

"1708, August 20th. Mr. Cheever died. The welfare of the Province was much upon his heart. *He abominated periwigs.*"

And so these people who took themselves so seriously must continue to be troubled about one another's habits and doings. As late as 1794 a law was passed to prohibit smoking "any pipe or cigar in any street, lane, or alley, under a penalty of two shillings," and the same penalty was assessed for "every duck or goose, gander or drake found in Frog pond."

When in March, 1766, the Stamp Act was repealed, a town meeting was called "by beat of drum and word of mouth." The town hall was illuminated, and six half-barrels of gunpowder were used.

This being an account of Newburyport's old churches, little more need be said of the town's part in the Revolution than that it was considerable. The records are full of the exploits of her citizens on land and sea, but particularly at sea. On receipt of the first news from Lexington, two days after the fight, the action of the people was not heroic. At a meeting called in the town house, in the midst of Thomas Cary's opening prayer, a messenger rushed upstairs calling out: "For God's sake, turn out! turn out! or you will all be killed! The regulars are marching this way and will soon be here. They are now at Ipswich, cutting and slashing all before them!" People rode through the streets crying, "Flee for your lives." One woman concealed all her pewter and silverware in the well, filled a bag with pies and other edibles and set off with her family. Eliphalet Hale of Exeter, who was at Ipswich, learning the report was false, rode from there to Newbury in fifty minutes.

Under date of September 27, 1801, we find the simple record:

"On this day, the reverend Thomas Cary preached for the last time in the meeting-house in Market square. The next day, the building was demolished, a well dug through the solid rock, and the town pump erected, near the spot where the pulpit formerly stood." And in October: "The new meeting-house, erected in Pleasant street, for the use of the first church and society, was this day dedicated. Sermon by the reverend John Andrews."

More than a hundred and fifty years had gone by since the little band landed on the banks of the Parker River—that stream which still winds so placidly through the marshes, rising and falling at its mouth with each tide. Five meetinghouses in the Old Town and one in Newburyport preceded this one which has already stood through six wars and escaped the great fire of 1811. Motor cars and trucks crowd the street where once merchants and farmers hitched their horses; but the beautiful old spire still looks down on the crowding roofs, still a landmark in the distance over land and sea.

XI

ST. JOHN'S, PORTSMOUTH, AND KITTERY, KENNEBUNK, AND PORTLAND IN THE STATE OF MAINE

OLD ST. JOHN'S at Portsmouth, though designed and built for an Episcopal church, is decidedly of the meetinghouse type. Still a prominent landmark from the Kittery shore and the harbor, it stands at the edge of the sidewalk facing some old houses at the top of the hill on Chapel Street—a site cold and wind-swept and rather bleak in winter. The monotony of the brick walls is only slightly relieved by the shallow breaks in the front and sides and by the two shallow arches. The stocky brick tower appears to be set upon the roof, though in reality its walls are carried down to form the vestibules, and the octagonal cupola with its delicate engaged Ionic columns, ornamented cornice, and many-lighted, round-headed windows is the only noteworthy feature of the exterior.

Inside, the galleries with their two orders of slender columns add to the meetinghouse effect; yet the interior has a good deal of charm and interest. Though the gray paint, here and there picked out with gilt, has been criticized by those who associate white woodwork with all buildings of the period, the color scheme is not without precedent and gives to the interior something of the "dim religious light" lacking in the too glaring white of most of the early meetinghouses.

Portsmouth's long past as a naval station and port is vividly recalled by the memorial tablets on the walls—many of them to young men of the colony who gave their lives for King and Country, as others since have given them for the same country without a king. One on the north wall is to the memory of the young midshipman Joshua Wentworth Larkin, who at the age of nineteen "lost his life in the active fulfilment of his duties and station on board the U.S. Ship Vincennes at Valparaiso." There are others to the memory of sailor sons or citizens of Portsmouth; among them, Captain Robert Forbes Bradford, Ensign Charles Emerson Hovey, killed in the Philippines in 1911, and (in the vestibule) Rear Admiral George Collier Remey and his wife.

The rectory is next to the church on the south side, a late eighteenth or early nineteenth century house, with mantels and other finish of the period. On the north is the old burying ground with tombs and graves of Governor Benning Wentworth and later New Hampshire governors and other notables. The iron doors of the row of old tombs open directly on the street.

The first clergyman of the Church of England to arrive at Strawberry Bank, as Portsmouth was then called, was Richard Gibson, who came from Saco, Maine. about 1640. In that year the first little English chapel and "parsonage house" were built, and a glebe was set apart. Though known as a "good scholar, a popular preacher and highly esteemed as gospel minister," Gibson was expelled four years later by the authorities of the Bay Colony for "denying its jurisdiction." His wife, before marriage, had been Mary Lewis of Saco; and he wrote to Governor Winthrop complaining that, "when she came from England some 2 years agoe, shee so behaued her selfe in the shipp, that the block was reaved at the mayne yard to have duckt her." Even though Mary was a lone lamb, unwelcome in the Puritan ark, she must have had some marked peculiarities to provoke treatment usually reserved for scolds and witches.

The settlement at Portsmouth was "distinctly Church of England," and the fishermen of the near-by Isles of Shoals who held out stubbornly against the Puritan authorities must have shared the feelings of Richard Vines of Saco, steward of Sir Ferdinando Gorges, who wrote to Governor Winthrop:

"I like Mr. Jenner [of Saco], his life and conversation, and also his preaching, if he would lett the Church of England alone; that doth much trouble me, to hear our mother Church questioned for her impurity vpon every occasion."

It was nearly a hundred years before the Church of England was finally established at Portsmouth. Meanwhile the Episcopalians' first little chapel, built in 1640, was used by the Congregationalists. A survival of that time is still observed in the title of "warden," continued in the Congregational church.

FAÇADE OF ST. JOHN'S CHURCH (1807) *Portsmouth, New Hampshire*

It was not until 1732 that the Queen's Chapel, named for George II's consort, Queen Caroline, was built on the site of the present church. Arthur Browne was the first rector: "a man of real culture, unpretentious goodness, and eminent worth." Son of an Irish family, he had been educated at Trinity College, Dublin. His son, Marmaduke Browne, became rector of Trinity Church at Newport.

Though the Portsmouth region had been settled first by people of the Church of England, Browne wrote in 1741, a few years after his coming to Portsmouth, that of the six or seven hundred families in the town and "district," only fifty to sixty were of the English Church, the rest being Independents.

It was Arthur Browne who somewhat reluctantly married Governor Benning Wentworth, on his sixtieth birthday, to his pretty young housemaid Martha Hilton, erstwhile drudge at the Earl of Halifax, as related by Longfellow, when the Governor

> said unto the Reverend Arthur Brown:
> "This is my birthday: it shall likewise be
> My wedding-day; and you shall marry me!"

But the Governor died not long afterward, and Martha would seem to have lost no time in seeking consolation, for she soon married his brother Michael, a retired officer in the British army, and it was the Reverend Arthur Browne, again, who married them. Both records are still to be seen in the parish register. And when some years later Mrs. Theodore Atkinson married John Wentworth, another New Hampshire governor and an early love, it was Arthur Browne who performed the ceremony, ten days after her first husband's funeral. This event had a sad ending for the then elderly clergyman, however, for as he "wanderd absent-mindedly" down the steps after the ceremony he fell and broke his arm. The record does not intimate any other cause contributing to this unfortunate accident; but, recalling the nature of the refreshments on such occasions and the liberality with which they were dispensed, we wonder.

It was to the little church of 1732 that President Washington came on his visit to New Hampshire just after his inauguration, sitting in the royal governor's old pew, with its red-plush cushions and heavy wooden canopy which had borne the royal arms. On this occasion the President is said to have worn a suit of black velvet with "brilliant buckles"; and with him was the "President of the State," General Sullivan. In the pew were the two chairs given by Queen Caroline. When, seventeen years later, the chapel was burned, and only one was saved, it was patriotically declared that that was the one the President had sat in. John Ogden was rector at the time of the President's visit.

After this first little church was burnt, on Christmas Eve, 1806, services were held for a time in the North Congregational Church. As St. John's was then without a rector, Dr. Buckminster, the pastor, officiated as reader and preacher. Later, when the South Church was without a minister the Episcopal rector served it as preacher for several months; and when in 1807 the present St. John's was finished (on the old site) the consecration service was shared by the Episcopal clergyman, Dr. Morss of Newburyport, and the minister of the South Church. We have seen a simliar amicable state of affairs about twenty-five years before, at King's Chapel in Boston.

At the close of the Revolution the American Episcopal Church had "neither legal existence, definite organization [nor] established forms." No candidate for holy orders could obtain them without swearing allegiance to the British Crown. The Church in America had no bishop, and for a time it seemed that Presbyterian ordination might be the only way in which it could recruit its clergy. After applying in vain for consecration in England as Bishop of Connecticut, Samuel Seabury at last received it in 1783 at the hands of the Scottish bishops, though the Church in Scotland had a scarcely legalized existence, since it had been suppressed on account of its adherence to the Stuart dynasty. Doubtless it was this state of things which caused some of the old animosities to be forgotten and brought the Episcopal and Congregational churches into more friendly relations.

Like Christ Church in Boston, St. John's has received some of the spoils of war. The bell was taken by Sir William Pepperell from a French church at the capture of Louisburg in 1745. It was cracked when the old church was burnt, and Paul Revere recast it. Worn by nearly another century of use, it was again recast in 1896 by Revere's successors.

The very old and curious font of porphyritic marble was given to the church by the two daughters of Colonel John Mason, who got it at the capture of Senegal from the French in 1758. It has been said, though questionably, that originally it had been taken from some heathen temple. The church has a Vinegar Bible given by Queen Caroline—one of the four pulpit Bibles in this country which have the typographical error of "vinegar" for "vineyard" in the title of the parable of the vineyard. Queen Caroline also gave the great folio prayer book to be seen in the vestibule of the church and the silver communion service and alms basin with the royal arms, now used only on special occasions. The famous "Brattle" organ, first used in King's Chapel in Boston, is in St. John's chapel, now the parish house, on State Street, where it was used until about 1900.

An old charity is still observed at St. John's Church, in its outward form at least. Colonel Theodore Atkinson, Sr., whose daughter-in-law married Governor John Wentworth, left the church a fund for providing a dole of twelve loaves of bread to be dispensed each Sunday to needy persons of the parish. This was a common form of charity in old English parishes. It is said that as much as $6,000 has been dispensed in the past in this way. The fund is still unimpaired, though it has long been merged with other parish endowments, and now on one Sunday each month the sexton simply places a loaf of bread on a table in the vestibule. For many years this has not been called for, and after the service he carries it home for his own use.

Writing of the early settlers of the Portsmouth region and the neighboring Maine coast, the Unitarian, Henry Foote said: "There is material for romance in these lives of Englishmen who kept alive their old-fashioned loyalty to Church and King, among uncongenial neighbors," neighbors who "would share no white surplice with Romish priests, but would minister in the scholar's black gown of Geneva," and who would not say the Lord's Prayer because it had been "superstitiously" used.

"The man of gentlest blood among these scattered Churchmen was Francis Campernowne, descended from a 'clarous and knightly family' " of Devonshire, nephew of Sir Ferdinando Gorges. An uncompromising and valiant leader, he had come in 1636 to the Maine and New Hampshire coasts, where he had inherited land at Kittery and York and on two of the near-by islands. He died in 1687 on Cutts Island, where on the monument over his grave is a sonnet with these concluding lines:

> Here rest the bones of Francis Campernowne;
>   The crest of Norman kings he bore.
> His fathers builded many a tower and town,
>   And ruled in England after Hastings' gore;
> Now o'er his grave the lonesome forests frown,
>   And sailless seas beat the untrodden shore.

At Kittery Point across the Piscataqua River, in Maine, is a little church well worth visiting for its architectural interest, but even more, perhaps, for the charm and beauty of its situation and surroundings. It was built in 1714—the same year as St. Michael's, Marblehead—and so it is among the oldest in New England. The interior, which probably was somewhat primitive at first—very likely a good deal like St. Michael's—has been somewhat modernized, though it still retains much of the character of the earlier New England meetinghouses. It is believed that the frame was cut and hewn in the vicinity of Dover and floated down the Piscataqua. Two of the original square pews with the small spindles in their backs, characteristic of the period, have been preserved, and the original pulpit and reading desk are still in place. Though the architectural motif with its crimson draperies is modern, it is in keeping with other details of the interior and adds much to its interest. This was the gift of the architect John Mead Howells (son of the writer, William Dean Howells), who lives at Kittery Point.

Originally the church faced west, but when in 1874 the old road was continued around the bend towards York, the building was turned about.

Kittery once included North and South Berwick and Eliot. Settled in 1623, it is the oldest town in Maine and is among the very earliest settlements in New England. It takes its name from a little hamlet in England. John Newmarch, a graduate of Harvard College, was the first minister. Though he was settled at Kittery as early as 1694 and at the Point only five years later, he was not ordained until the year the church was built, 1714. He served the parish until within three years of his death in 1754—fifty-two years.

All of this region is historic. Next to the church is the Sparhawk house, built by Sir William Pepperell for his son-in-law and daughter, and the Commodore Stephen Decatur house is near by.

The old shipbuilding town of Kennebunk is a place of quiet, elm-shaded streets and many fine old houses, once the homes of prosperous shipowners and retired sea captains.

Except for the steeple, wherein hangs one of Paul Revere's bells, the exterior of Kennebunk's old church is quite plain and unadorned. In the tower and belfry, however, we have one more example of the seemingly unlimited number of agreeable compositions possible with different combinations of the same familiar elements. In this case the small cupola surmounts an octagonal story, with the clock face in a somewhat unusual position above the belfry.

The original building, now the First Parish Church of Kennebunk, was erected in 1773. Thirty years later the membership had so increased that it had to be enlarged by the usual method of sawing it in two and moving back the rear section. The belfry was built then, and probably it was about this time that the old square pews with hinged seats and headrests were taken out. The slip pews that took their place still have the hinged doors. Today they have red cushions, which, with the red carpets on the aisles, and the red damask draperies behind the old high pulpit give the ever desirable touch of color to the interior. Beautiful old chandeliers light the church.

A church was organized in Kennebunk in 1744, and the first little meetinghouse was built at the "Landing." Parts of this old building were used in the present church.

Citizens of the state of Maine will tell you that the earliest settlers landed on the Maine coast nearly twenty years before the settlement at Plymouth. The first permanent settlement at Kennebunkport (called Arundel then, and until 1820) was made as early as 1629 by Richard Vines. In 1650 a community was established farther inland on the site of the present village of Kennebunk, then part of Wells. For nearly half a century the village was in constant dread of attacks by the Indians. Daniel Little was the first pastor, and he served Kennebunk faithfully for fifty years.

Ships were built on the Mousam River as early as 1730, but it

FIRST PARISH CHURCH (1773) *Kennebunk, Maine*

was about a hundred years later that the great era of shipbuilding began in Kennebunk.

Most famous was the four-masted ship *Ocean King,* 2,516 tons, launched in 1874. The last ship built in the Thompson yard was the *Reuce,* 1,900 tons, in 1881. She was in service until 1922, when she was wrecked on the coast of Japan.

Among other Kennebunk masters and owners or part owners were the Lords, the Kingsburys, the Titcombs, and the Williamses. From 1801 to 1861 the Williamses were principal owners or masters of nearly thirty different ships. On the Sunday after their return from their long voyages, we can see these men with their wives and families walking down the aisle of the old church. In blue tail coat with brass buttons and fawn-colored trousers, tall beaver hat in hand, they take their places at the head of the pew. And at the door after the service, friends and neighbors gather round with questions as to the success of the voyage. How did the new bark handle? And was there much damage in the September gale off Hatteras?

In 1848 a lock was built at the narrows on the Kennebunk River to provide deep water for the larger ships built in the yards above. The warping of a large vessel down the stream was an anxious time for the builder. Jesse Towne was pilot of all the big ships built at the Landing. Familiar with every turn of the river, with a big crew of men on each bank to warp the vessel along, he planned in advance the best course to follow. Towne would stand on the deck, dancing up and down with excitement and shouting orders at the top of his voice. "Pull! Pull, boys, pull all together! There she goes right into the bank, in the mud, can't get her off, have to wait till next tide. Heave ho! See if you can't start her again!" So he would run on, probably with much additional sea language, as the clerical president of a New England college used to say, "unfit for a layman's ears." But Towne was a good pilot and always got his ships safely down.

When Kennebunk meetinghouse was enlarged, nearly a century and a half ago, it was said to have "excelled in beauty and symmetry" any other in Maine; and indeed, for the period when it was built, the same perhaps might be said today. At any rate, then it was the pride of the village, though without doubt its builders would be shocked at the more liberal views of its present-day congregations, for they voted that no orations were to be delivered in it.

One more of Paul Revere's bells still hangs in the belfry. Three times a day—at seven o'clock, at noon, and at nine for the curfew—it was regularly rung until the coming of the factories with their bells and whistles. At evening, the last ringing was followed by strokes indicating the days of the month. The tone was remarkably strong and clear; at the time of the disastrous fire in Kennebunk in 1824 it was heard in the town of Alfred, eleven miles way. Today, plain to be seen by travelers on the Boston and Portland road, it still rings out its Sunday morning call to service.

Three or four miles down the river is the village of Kennebunkport. Here are another eighteenth century meetinghouse and some fine old houses and picturesque shipyards.

Portland has an old church of considerable interest, and although there are of course other fine old churches and meetinghouses in Maine, we shall end our journey there.

Built of Freeport granite, the Church of the First Parish in Portland would be notable among New England churches of the Colonial and Federal periods on account of its material if for no other reason. King's Chapel had been built of Quincy granite seventy-five years before, but on all our travels these are the only two stone churches of the early periods which we have found.

The first settler on the site of Portland is believed to have been Christopher Levett, who built a stone house, and here he and others with him spent the winter of 1623–24. In 1628 Captain Levett was appointed by royal commission as Governor of New England, and authorized to raise contributions in England "to build a city there and call it York"; but he died before anything of the kind was accomplished. Various other hardy adventurers followed during the first half of the seventeenth century. During these years there seem to have been continual disputes with Sir Ferdinando Gorges, the proprietor of Maine, until the region came under the control of Massachusetts in 1652. Gorges had made a settlement at Saco in 1636, and about that time Richard Gibson preached there and at near-by Casco, where he established the first church in Maine before going to Ports-

THE ORGAN LOFT, FIRST PARISH CHURCH *Portland, Maine*

INTERIOR, FIRST PARISH CHURCH (1825) *Portland, Maine*

mouth. Gibson was followed at Casco by Robert Jordan, described as "an itinerant preacher" of the English Church and as "the soul of the opposition to Massachusetts, for which, and for baptising children, he was more than once arrested."

Most of the early settlers in Maine had no sympathy with Puritanism; but some time before 1675 a meetinghouse was built on the "Neck," as the early settlement at Portland was called. Later the place was known as Falmouth, and here came George Burroughs, one of the "itinerant preachers" who for seventy years served the people of this region. In 1692 Burroughs was hanged for a witch on Gallows Hill at Salem. "Although the spectators at his hanging," says Adams, "were so moved as almost to prevent the sentence from being carried out, Mather, who was witnessing the spectacle from horseback, told the people that the victim was not an ordained clergyman, and that, in any case, the devil often appeared as an Angel of Light." Burroughs had received his A.B. degree at Harvard at the age of twenty. Although he was not ordained until six years after he preached at Falmouth, it must have been generally known that he had been ordained at Danvers, where in 1680 he had been minister of the Congregational Church; and Mather's statement to the crowd at the execution would seem to have been deliberately untrue.

During King Philip's War Falmouth was attacked by the Indians, and the inhabitants were driven out. No permanent settlement was established again until sometime after 1716. A church was organized about five years later, and the first Falmouth meetinghouse was built at the corner of Middle and India streets. This little building was used until 1746. For a while after a new church was built the old one was used as a town house, and sessions of the court were held here; but the building was burnt when fire swept the town during Mowatt's bombardment in 1775. It was about this time that Falmouth was renamed Portland, for that great limestone headland on the southern coast of England, famous as the source of Portland stone.

The second church, long known as "Old Jerusalem," was built in 1740 on the site of the present building on Congress Street. Though damaged by Mowatt's guns, it survived the fire and stood until the present church was built, having once been enlarged by the usual method of cutting apart; in this case by moving a section on each side of the pulpit. For nearly a hundred years it was a prominent landmark in Portland. The young Longfellow wrote a poem protesting its destruction.

The present stone church was built in 1825. On careful examination it may be noticed that the cut stone finish of one of the windows on the east side is different from that of other stone trim. It seems that a strike among the stonecutters was threatened —more promptly dealt with perhaps in those days than now— and some Chelmsford stone was obtained from the Charlestown, Massachusetts, State Prison. Admirers of the church take pride in the fact that no professional architect had anything to do with it. Certainly it was built in an age, then unfortunately nearing its end, when a knowledge and appreciation of architectural design was still existent among the cultured inhabitants and the craftsmen of American communities; and if the First Parish Church of Portland does not take first rank among New England churches and meetinghouses of the period, it certainly is a creditable piece of work for amateur architects.

Unfortunately the interior has not escaped some of the nineteenth century "improvements" which most of our old churches suffered. Originally the mahogany "pillars" that carried the arch were connected with the galleries by false fronts on the wall. Charles Codman is said to have offered to paint sitters in these blind galleries, and for an additional fee to change the ladies' bonnets from time to time in accordance with prevailing styles. In 1855 the wooden columns supporting the galleries were replaced with iron ones, the arch and columns of the pulpit recess were torn out, and the walls "decorated" in accordance with the fashion of the time. The fine crystal chandelier was the gift of ten friends of the parish at the time the church was built. The cannon ball at the top was lodged in the wall of the older church when Mowatt bombarded the town.

It was during the pastorate of Ichabod Nichols that the church attained its greatest prominence. In 1809, yielding to the prevailing sentiment of the times, it became Unitarian.

Portland today is a pleasant city with many historic old houses and some fine modern buildings. At intervals of about a hundred years during the three centuries since it was settled, the town has suffered three staggering disasters. Devastated by the Indians in

King Philip's War, it was burnt by the British at the beginning of the Revolution; and again in 1866 it was swept by flames.

Early in 1775, Captain Mowatt of the British sloop-of-war *Canceau* with a companion was strolling about the town and was seized by some Colonials who decided that he was spying upon them. On his promise to return when requested, he was released on parole—a promise which he kept, but not by request. In October he returned with four ships and demanded the surrender of all arms of every kind in the possession of the inhabitants. Upon their refusal, he opened fire on the morning of the 18th, pouring shells and grenades into the defenseless town. St. Paul's Church, all the public buildings, and three-quarters of the houses were burnt to the ground; and a thousand men, women, and children were homeless at the beginning of winter.

Among the few buildings saved was the widow Grele's tavern, and here, for the duration of the war, the county court was held. The old tavern stood until some time in the present century.

Like many of the older churches in cities and towns which were placed on sites once adequate and convenient, the old First Parish Church of Portland now is overshadowed by the modern high buildings of Congress Street. Yet, even so, if members of the old building committee could see their work today they might well feel that their aim as stated in their final report had been accomplished: to erect a structure "which would continue to be an object of peculiar regard to the present and to future generations." Indeed, it seems now as though, except for some calamity of war or conflagration or a yielding by its proprietors to the lure of large profit from the value of the site, the old granite building might well stand for centuries, in time to become venerated and respected among the most venerable and historic of old New England meetinghouses.

XII

CONCLUSION

For centuries the spire of the village church has been traditional; ever a marked feature of the landscape, a "silent finger of faith pointing to the home of the faithful." Though the chief desire of the emigrating Puritan apparently was to leave behind him every ornament, every reminder, of the hated English Church and all connected with it, the one exception seems to have been the meetinghouse bell and the "turret" to hang it in—before many years to be developed into the church spire, or "steeple."

To the European coming to our shores, after the first amazing spectacle of the towering sky line of our great cities, few things can seem more strange than the rather meager wooden architecture of our smaller towns and villages, and particularly of the churches. Yet, as we have seen, for many years they were the logical product of the most available materials and methods of construction, as to some extent they are still.

For hundreds of years, in the old country they left behind, and in the rural districts especially, the parish church was the center, not only for the religious devotions for which it was consecrated, but of community life of every kind. In the New World they called them meetinghouses, and meeting houses in truth they were, and still are. "There the past and present meet. The very thresholds are worn by vanished feet, the pews recall those who once sat in them, memories walk softly up the aisles."

In this present land of numberless creeds and churches, it is hard to realize that day, not much more than a hundred years ago, when in many a community there was but one church and that one was entirely under the authority of the town government, whose clerk kept the records which are the source of our knowledge of its early history.

What is to be the ultimate fate of some of these old churches?

Most of those that have survived are still in use, and in our larger towns and cities they usually have large and devoted congregations, aware of their historic associations and intrinsic beauty; conscious of an obligation to keep and maintain them and to pass them on, a sacred trust for the benefit of future generations. Yet, as we have seen, some are abandoned, or in use as town halls or picture houses. Let us hope that most of them will continue to stand, for, if civilization as we have known it is to survive, it can only be by a return to the original ideals of this country, inseparable from the old moral and spiritual standards of the Christian churches.

There are of course those who think that nothing that belongs to the past is of consequence; that our only interest should be with the present, with rather less concern, perhaps, for the future. But we have gained nothing to take the place of what we have lost through the discarding of tradition, and there are still those who believe we may enjoy the wonders of the present age without accepting the dictates of an age that would break with everything that is past.

The legend of the Sibylline Books is as much a truism today as ever; how in Rome, long before the days of the Caesars, there came to the King a mysterious woman, offering him nine ancient volumes filled with prophecies. The price she asked was a king's ransom—no less. The King declined to buy them, and the woman went away. Having burned three of the books, she came again and offered the six remaining for the same price as the original nine. Again the King refused, and again the woman departed, but presently returned with only three of the volumes which she once more offered at the price of the nine. Whereupon the King was troubled; and, taking council of his advisers as to what he should do, he bought the remaining three books for the price of the nine. Which is an allegory: that, though that which is plentiful may be dear, that which is scarce may become priceless. To which an English writer, Aymer Vallance, adds:

"It is impossible to over-estimate the importance of systematic study of the priceless and ever-diminishing treasures of the past. For to study is to acquire appreciation; and to appreciate is to realize the paramount obligation of preserving with most scrupulous care that which has come down to us, in order to hand on this precious heritage intact to posterity. Foremost among repositories of antiquity are the fabrics and fittings of our historic parish churches, venerable and lovely still in spite of the many devastating changes that have swept over them."

REFERENCES

Adams, James Truslow: *The Founding of New England*

Babcock, Mrs. Samuel G.: *Christ Church, Boston*

Bacon, Edwin M.: *Rambles Around Old Boston*

Bacon, Oliver N.: *History of Natick*

Bliss, William Root: *Side Glimpses from the Colonial Meeting-House*

Booth, Vincent Ravi: "Restoration of the Old First Church of Bennington, Vermont," in *Old Time New England* (bulletin of the Society for the Preservation of New England Antiquities), Jan. 1940

Clark, George L.: *A History of Connecticut*

Coffin, Joshua: *History of Newbury, Newburyport and West Newbury*

Cox, Charles J.: *English Church Fittings, Furniture and Accessories*

Crawford, Mary Caroline: *The Romance of Old New England Churches*

——: *St. Botolph's Town*

Cutter, Daniel B.: *History of the Town of Jaffrey, New Hampshire*

Cutting, Alfred Wayland: *Old Time Wayland*

Drake, Samuel G.: *History and Antiquities of Boston*

Drake, Samuel Adams: *Nooks and Corners of the New England Coast*

Earle, Alice Morse: *The Sabbath in Puritan New England*

Elliott, Maud Howe: *This Was My Newport*

Federal Writers' Project Guides: *Maine. New Hampshire. Vermont. Massachusetts. Rhode Island. Connecticut*

Fiske, John: *The American Revolution*

Fogg, Mary Putnam: *Old Trinity Church and the Malbone Family*

Foote, Henry Wilder: *Annals of King's Chapel*

Forbes, Allan: *Towns of New England and Old England* (published by the State Street Trust Company)

Forbes, Esther: *Paul Revere and the World He Lived in*

Green, John Richard: *A Short History of the English People*

Greene, Louise: "Kennebunk Meeting-House," in *Historic Churches and Homes of Maine,* by Maine Writers Research Club

Hayward, Willis: *History of Hancock, New Hampshire*

Hudson, Alfred Sereno: *History of Sudbury*

Jenkins, Stephen: *The Old Boston Post Road*

Johnson, Alexander: *Connecticut*

Kelly, J. Frederick: "A Forgotten Incident in the Life of Ithiel Town," and "Raising Connecticut Meeting-Houses," in *Old Time New England* (bulletin of the Society for the Preservation of New England Antiquities), Jan., 1941, and July, 1936

Macaulay, Thomas Babington: *Critical and Historical Essays. History of England*

Marvin, Abijah P.: *History of the Town of Lancaster, Mass.*

McCulloch, Samuel Clyde: "Foundation and Early Work of the Society for the Propagation of the Gospel in Foreign Parts," in *Huntington Library Quarterly,* May, 1945

Metcalf, John G.: *Annals of the Town of Mendon*

Orcutt, William Dana: *From My Library Walls*

Perkins, John Carroll: *Annals of King's Chapel* (Vol. III)

Place, Charles A.: "From Meeting House to Church in New England," in *Old Time New England,* Oct., 1922, Jan., Apr., July, 1923

Place, Charles A.: "The Bulfinch Church, Lancaster, Mass.," in *Architectural Forum,* June, 1921

Roads, Samuel, Jr.: *History and Traditions of Marblehead*

Robinson, Rowland E.: *Vermont*

Sewall, Samuel, *Diary*

Speare, Eva A.: *Colonial Meeting-Houses of New Hampshire*

Temple, Josiah H.: *History of Framingham, Mass.*

Thompson, Margaret J.: *Captain Nathaniel Lord Thompson of Kennebunk*

Todd, Charles Burr: *In Olde Connecticut*

Train, Arthur: *Puritan's Progress*

Treves, Sir Frederick: *Highways and Byways in Dorset*

Van de Water, Frederick F.: *The Reluctant Republic*

Walker, George Leon: *Thomas Hooker, Preacher, Founder, Democrat*

Ward, Elizabeth: *Old Times in Shrewsbury*

Weis, Frederick Lewis: *The Colonial Clergy and the Colonial Churches of New England*

Winthrop (Hannah) Chapter of the Daughters of the American Revolution: *An Historic Guide to Cambridge*

Wolkins, G. G.: *Freedom and the Old South Meeting-House* (Old South Leaflets)